Cork in Old Photographs

Tim Cadogan

GILL & MACMILLAN

Gill & Macmillan Ltd
Hume Avenue
Park West
Dublin 12
with associated companies throughout the world
www.gillmacmillan.ie

© 2003 Tim Cadogan
0 7171 3566 7
Design and print origination by O'K Graphic Design, Dublin
Printed by ColourBooks Ltd, Dublin

The paper used in this book is made from the wood pulp of managed forests.
For every tree felled, at least one tree is planted, thereby renewing natural resources.

A catalogue record is available for this book from the British Library.

3 5 6 4 2

Contents

Acknowledgments

The compilation of a collection of photographs is dependent on the cooperation and good will of many people.

I wish to acknowledge my gratitude to the following organisations and individuals who gave me access to their archives and collections and gave permission to reproduce photographs:

Cork City Library (and Local Studies Librarian Kieran Burke); the *Irish Examiner* (and librarian Anne Kearney); Cork County Library; Colman O'Mahony; Angela McCarthy; Henry Ford & Son, Ltd., Cork (and Anne O'Leary); Tom Trehy; Gerry Lewis and John L. O'Sullivan.

Thanks are also due to the following for their expertise and assistance: Peggy Sue Amiston, Denis McSweeney Photo Shop, Kieran Wyse, Richard Henchion, Colman O'Mahony, Aodh Ó Tuama, Brian Magee and Colin Rynne. Special thanks to Helen and Ross.

Introduction

About Cork

The name of Cork describes its location. It is derived from the Irish *Corcach*, meaning a bog or marshy area; scarcely an appropriate place to build a city in ordinary circumstances. The land on which the city developed was in olden times broken into islands by the meandering streams of the River Lee. It is protected north and south by steep hills and it was on its southern slopes near Gillabbey that Finbarr's monastery was founded in the seventh century.

The foundations of the city were laid in later centuries by Norsemen, scavengers turned settlers, along the axis that later became the South and North Main streets. This, with some sideways expansion, formed the nucleus of the Norman city which was granted a charter in 1185, an event celebrated as the official birth of the city by the Cork 800 celebrations of 1985. This was a walled city which in the fourteenth century enclosed an area of thirty-six acres. Outside the walls the native Irish began to settle over time, beginning to populate the lower slopes to the north and south, where fortifications and monastic houses also developed in the medieval period. The walled town was built on an island and was surrounded by other islands. These islands or marshes were gradually drained and built upon and were linked by bridges.

Early eighteenth-century Cork was Venice-like, with waterways serving as streets and with steps leading up from quaysides to the entrances of trading houses. Examples of these steps survive in the South Mall and in Patrick Street. The next stage of urban improvement, which occurred in the second half of the eighteenth century and the early years of the nineteenth century, was the covering over of these waterways and the creation of the modern street network of the city centre.

The development of Cork was fuelled by a flourishing provision trade. Cork earned the reputation of being 'the slaughterhouse of Ireland' from the vast quantities of cattle and pigs slaughtered in the city and salted for export. The butter export trade from Cork was also of international significance. In addition to the provision trades and spin-offs such as tanning and coopering, Cork had successful brewing, distilling and textile industries.

The circumstances of Cork's development have conspired to produce a city that today has scarcely a fragment remaining of the medieval city and little of the sixteenth- and seventeenth-century city. The modern city centre, essentially of eighteenth century origin, found its modern layout and appearance in the nineteenth century.

Change is the natural order of urban streetscapes. In Cork's case the normal gradual change was accelerated by events. The burning of Cork by rampaging Black and Tans in 1920 destroyed a large sector of Patrick Street; its reconstruction did not however result in any radical reordering of the street. Likewise, despite the luxury of a decade to consider it, City Hall, also a victim of the 1920 fires, was rebuilt on its old site. More radical renewal was achieved in the gradual clearance of the city's slums and the rehousing over a long period of their inhabitants in artisan dwelling developments and in the 1930s by the building of the Gurranebraher suburb.

About the photographs

There are surviving photographs that document many of the changes that time has wrought in the city. Very often, however, the image has become separated from the contexts of time and photographer. For assistance in approximating dates of photographs I have relied on published histories, on postal and trade directories and on previously published photographic compilations. If on occasion I have erred, I cannot blame my sources.

In recent decades photographs have become an increasingly valued adjunct to local studies research. There are indeed aspects of the past that cannot be adequately researched without some photographic or visual evidence. Urban architecture and the streetscapes of a century ago are, for example, topics particularly enhanced by photographic research. A photograph may not always be worth a thousand words, but in the hands of a keen-eyed observer it can become a primary source document of great worth.

The photographs gathered in this volume do not aspire to be an illustrated history of the city. They span the century from 1860 to 1960 and attempt to provide a balance between the idealised topographical photographs associated with postcard views and photographs illustrating everyday life in the city. However, surviving photographs of the past as reflected in local archives and collections are predominantly topographical or event-focused in subject. To illustrate the deficit: though horses abound in street views of nineteenth-century Cork, I have failed to locate a photograph of the stables where they were kept. I am sure that a wealth of photographic material survives in attics and drawers and will hopefully surface in the future to enlarge the range of our photographic heritage.

About photography in Cork

Most of the photographs reproduced here are credited to anonymous photographers, though a significant number can be given a corporate identity. The output of Cork's pioneering photographers from the 1860s onwards is not, to my knowledge, widely represented in named collections in photographic archives. They included a number of commercial photographers. From 1863 to 1900 the number of photographic studios listed in Cork trade directories ranged between seven and eleven. Earlier listings in that period included some who were also miniature painters, and portraiture was emphasised by most of those advertising their services. Timothy J. Callaghan, who opened his Portrait Rooms in 1863, provided advice on attire for patrons: 'Ladies are informed that dark silk or satin, shot, watered, or plain, produce pleasing effects; also checked and figured materials, provided they are not too light.' Despite his focus on portraiture, however, Callaghan also advertised for sale his 'Twenty-one Views of Cork and Environs' at 2/6 each or £2.5s for the set.

Francis Guy, later Guy & Co. Ltd, of 70 Patrick Street, was Cork's leading photographic firm for many years. It was also the city's leading printer and publisher. As publisher of historical and touring guides and of annual directories, Guy's amassed a huge collection of photographic plates, but regrettably this potentially invaluable collection is said to have been inadvertently destroyed when they moved premises in the 1960s. A number of photographs by the firm are reproduced from printed sources in this collection.

Photography as historical record made a significant advance when newspapers began to use the medium in their publications. The *Cork Examiner* had published photographs irregularly from the early 1900s, and from 1911 included a daily photographic section. Thomas Barker (d. 1925) of the *Cork Examiner* was one of the pioneers of press photography in Ireland, and another Cork-born press photographer of note, Joseph Cashman, worked at both Guy's and the *Cork Examiner* before moving to Dublin. A number of photographs from the *Examiner* archive are included in this volume.

Photography was of course a field in which amateur practitioners excelled. Humphrey Haines, a Grand Parade apothecary, was a photographer active in the 1850s. Several of his photographs are reproduced in Edward Chandler's *Photography in Ireland; the nineteenth century* (Dublin, 2001). Thomas R. Lane, the brewer, was another gentleman photographer and he photographed the demolition of the old St Fin Barre's cathedral in 1862. The product of this early photo-history project was published in 1866 under the title *Vetusta Monumenta Coragiae, being nine views of the late Cathedral of S. Fin Barre's, Cork*; it was revisited in a recent article (Rynne and Wigham, *JCHAS*, 2002).

The Cork Camera Club was formed in 1923 for 'the promotion of Photography'. Its Secretary and Treasurer was Alec R. Day of the noted Cork family. Members met fortnightly and went on summer outings to places of scenic and archaeological interest. A collection of their photographs was donated to Cork City Library in 1938, along with a number of older photographs presented by Alec Day. A number of these photographs are reproduced in this compilation.

The 'Beautiful city, charming and pretty' of Cork's alternative anthem has probably changed more in the past generation than in the previous century. It has perhaps lost some of its intimacy in the pursuit of progress. The reordering of Patrick Street that is currently being undertaken may help to redress the balance. One is struck when perusing old photographs not by the leisurely pace of life that they reflect, but by the ability that past times afforded to stop and observe one's surroundings. One of the pleasures of looking at old photographs is the awareness of our surroundings that they awaken in us in our everyday perambulations. Nowadays streetscapes and urban vistas are rendered 'invisible' by traffic, parked vehicles and the frenetic pace of life. Our gaze is arrested by modern shop fronts and we ignore the upper floors of their buildings. Look up, history is often visible at rooftop level!

Cork in
Old Photographs

Fr Mathew Statue

Fr Mathew has presided over Patrick Street since 1864; the statue by John Henry Foley was unveiled on the 74th anniversary of Fr Mathew's birth. The unveiling ceremony, performed by the Mayor, John Francis Maguire, was an enormous event, attended by an estimated 100,000 people. Fr Mathew, a Capuchin Friar and a native of Thomastown, Co. Tipperary, came to Cork in 1814. Though nationally hailed as the Apostle of Temperance, in Cork Fr Mathew was also remembered for his work during the cholera epidemic of 1832 and for his establishment of St Joseph's Cemetery.

General view of Cork

Around 1900, an enterprising member of Guy's photographic staff chose the high ground to the north-west of the city as vantage point for a spectacular view of the city. This photograph shows the view to the east. To the extreme left is the tower of St Mary's Cathedral, in the middle-distance is St Anne Shandon and on the right the Lee winds its way towards the harbour. Only St Patrick's Bridge spans the visible part of the north channel. The substantial building in the foreground is Maymount House, residence during the last century of O'Connell, O'Leary and Ó Tuama families; it was demolished in the 1970s.

General View of Cork

General view of Cork (from Gillabbey)

The vantage point for this unusual general view of Cork is Gillabbey, a location midway between UCC and St Finbarre's Cathedral. The south channel of the Lee at Gillabbey Weir is in the foreground, crossed in the middle distance by the Cork and Muskerry Light Railway bridge. The Cork terminus of the line was located in Bishop's Marsh, a portion of which is located on the right. The railway line closed in 1934. Bishop's Marsh is now the site of Jury's Hotel.

Fr Mathew's Grave

This photograph, published in a religious magazine, the *Irish Rosary*, in 1902, shows Fr Mathew's grave in St Joseph's Cemetery, Ballyphehane, in what were then the southern suburbs of Cork city. The cross over his grave commemorates the opening of the cemetery by Fr Mathew in 1830. He bought the cemetery, formerly the Botanic Gardens, to provide a burial ground for the poor and so that Catholics could be buried without the threat of Protestant interference. Fr Mathew was interred beneath the cross at his own request in December 1856.

General view of Cork (to the south)

This detail from the photographer's north-west vantage point shows the view to the south *c.* 1900. This view, looking over the roofs of Blarney Street, is dominated by St Finbarre's Cathedral. In the lower left corner in the near distance is the Mercy Hospital, incorporating the old Mansion House, built in 1767 to the design of Davis Ducart. From 1847 it served as a Diocesan College administered by the Vincentians, before commencing its modern function as Ireland's first Mercy Hospital on 17 March 1857.

Fr Mathew Centenary 1956
The centenary of the death of Fr Mathew in 1956 was celebrated in Cork by a massive procession of Pioneers from the city to the Mardyke, where they were addressed by Bishop Cornelius Lucey, who concelebrated open-air mass. Fr James, OFM Cap, delivered the oration. The photograph shows Garda Pioneers marching through Patrick Street in the procession. In the background can be seen the façade of Roches Stores.

Irish National Foresters
The Irish National Foresters (INF) was founded in Dublin in 1877 as a benefit society to provide relief for members and their families. It originally had links with the IRB and was strongly nationalist in outlook. Each branch of the INF, of which there were several in Cork city, was led by a Chief Ranger and Sub-Chief Ranger. This photograph shows the INF contingent preceded by three horsemen and a float carrying their colourful banner as they pass Grant's in Patrick Street during a parade around 1910.

Corporation Carriage

An official presence at the St Patrick's Day parade was *de rigeur* by 1914. This photograph shows the carriage bearing the principal Corporation dignitaries. The four occupants are, from left: Cllr Daniel Horgan (*in loco* the Lord Mayor), Cllr Richard H. Tilson (City High Sheriff), Ald Cors Mullany and Mr Barry C. Galvin (City Solicitor). On the driver's seat, but out of picture, was the City Sword Bearer in full regalia.

St Patrick's Day Parade 1914

Mass participation in parades has declined in recent decades, but a century ago parades were both an entertainment and a medium of expression for thousands of citizens. St Patrick's Day parades were enthusiastically organised and supported, as is evidenced in this photograph of portion of the parade featuring the Barrack Street No. 1 Band passing through Patrick Street. The man alone on the pavement seems unimpressed by the spectacle. The business premises on the right of the photo are Lambkin Bros., tobacco manufacturers and Simcox, grocers.

Parade Committee

The parade route was from Washington Street, *via* North Gate Bridge, Camden Quay, Patrick Street and Grand Parade to the National Monument where an oration was given. The 1914 parade featured 16 bands. This photograph is of the marshals who organised and conducted the event. On the right in Forester's regalia is the chief marshal, J.J. Sheridan, on the left is Brian Boru (performed by D. O'Regan) and centre front is V. Rev. Thomas, O.S.F.C., who gave the oration. Brian Boru's role in the event remains a mystery!

Statue of George II

Cork's Grand Parade has the curious Irish name of 'Sráid an Chapaill Bhuídhe' (Street of the White Horse), but the origin of the name is explained by this and the following photograph, which depict the equestrian statue of George II mounted on a white horse. The statue, popularly called 'George a' horseback', was executed by John van Nost and originally placed on Tuckey Bridge in the centre of Grand Parade in 1761. It was moved to its final location at the southern end of the Parade when the Grand Parade waterway was covered over.

National Monument

This postcard photograph shows the Cork National Monument at the southern end of Grand Parade near the site previously occupied by the George II statue. The National Monument, 'erected to perpetuate the memories of the men of 1798, 1803, 1848, and 1867', was inspired by the 1798 centenary commemoration, though not unveiled until St Patrick's Day 1906. The monument was commissioned by the Cork Young Ireland Society and was designed by D.J. Coakley. The central figure of Erin and those of Tone, Dwyer, Davis and O'Neill Crowley at the corners were executed by John F. Davis. The monument was unveiled by the 1798 historian Fr Kavanagh.

Statue of George II (2)

By 1862, the monarch had difficulty in retaining his seat and required a prop to prevent him falling over. On the night of 3 March 1862, George II toppled over, with, it was suggested, some assistance from an unadmiring prankster. George was broken in several pieces and 'all the King's men' couldn't put him together again. A few weeks later the horse was removed from its plinth and, according to press reports, was to be melted down, but the head was salvaged and survives in England.

Lady in Black/Grand Parade

This photograph dates from about 1906 and shows a fashionable lady of indeterminate age dressed entirely in black posing for the photographer against the backdrop of the western side of the Grand Parade. The girls crossing the Parade behind her seem to be dressed for a less austere day than the main figure. The premises behind the lady in black, Fieldings, Electrical Engineers, occupied the site on which Cork City Library now stands.

Grand Parade, 1872

The two horse-drawn trams in view date this photograph of the Grand Parade to the years 1872–74, during which the city had a horse tram system. Behind the tram on the left, the English Market presents a low street frontage. Gibson, in his *History of Cork* (1861), remarked that 'the houses on the Parade are even more irregular than those on Patrick Street'. This defect was remedied in the case of the English Market in 1884, when a new and more elevated entrance was built.

Dún Mhuire

This photograph, *c.* 1960, shows the attractive building at the riverside end of the Grand Parade, then known as Dún Mhuire. Originally called Daly's Clubhouse and later the City Club, it dates from around 1787, but was extensively altered and refaced to the design of Sir John Benson. In 1952, the City Club having amalgamated with the County Club at the latter's South Mall premises, this building was purchased at auction for £9,125 by the Legion of Mary for use as its Diocesan headquarters. It was officially opened as Dún Mhuire on 7 December 1952. In more recent times, it has become a financial business premises.

Grand Parade, 1900s

This Reliable Series postcard view of the Grand Parade in the first decade of the twentieth century illustrates another stage in the evolution of public transport. Here an electric tram approaches the Berwick Fountain. The fountain was erected in 1860 by Walter Berwick in remembrance of the twelve years he had spent in Cork as chairman of the quarter sessions and was designed by Sir John Benson. Prior to the filling in of the waterway on the Parade in the 1780s, the channel was bridged at this point by Tuckey's Bridge.

Singer's/Finn's Corners

This photograph, dating from *c.* 1890, is taken on Grand Parade, but its focal point is the junction of Grand Parade with Great George's Street (now Washington Street). An interesting feature of the photograph is that the two premises in the centre of the photograph, the Singer Manufacturing Co. on the left and the clothing store on the right, are still in operation today more than a century later. Indeed, several generations of Corkonians have known these corners as Singer's Corner and Finn's Corner.

United Ireland Rally, 1933

This *Irish Press* photograph of 1 October 1933 shows the crowd at a United Ireland rally in Grand Parade. The rally, which attracted an estimated 25,000 people, was viewed with concern by the authorities, as the Anti-Imperialist League, an IRA group, announced a rival meeting. This concern prompted a large Garda presence, supplemented by military, a steel-helmeted squad of whom are pictured in a Crossley tender in the left foreground. The United Ireland rally was addressed by General O'Duffy and other speakers in Grand Parade, while the rival meeting was addressed by Tom Barry and others a short distance away in South Mall. The proceedings passed off peacefully.

Grand Parade, 1940
This postcard view of the Grand Parade, *c.* 1940, takes in the full length of the Parade, from the riverside foreground to Daunt's Square in the background. The buses in this photograph (as well as the motor cars) mark the arrival of the street traffic with which we are familiar today. Despite the motor traffic, this view gives a good impression of the width of Grand Parade, which is indeed the widest thoroughfare in the city.

Washington Street, looking west
This London-published postcard view of Washington Street from the Grand Parade postdates 1918, in which year the Corporation honoured the first President of the USA by renaming Great George's Street in his honour. When originally opened by the Wide Street Commissioners in 1824, this was called New Road, but was officially named Great George's Street in honour of the reigning monarch. The north side of the street was built first; the opposite side commencing a few years later. The Deane family of architectural fame was associated with the development of the street.

Washington Street, looking east

This Cork Photocard views Washington Street from the opposite end. The classical façade of the courthouse, which at this time had an iron railing surround, frames the left side of the photo; the façade of Dwyer's warehouse, built in 1874, is on the right. Two trams share the roadway with a variety of horse-drawn vehicles. The cable bracket arm carrying the overhead electric cable for the trams is visible in the foreground. The terminus of trams on this route was at Sunday's Well.

Courthouse

The imposing Classical portico of the City and County Courthouse features in this Guy's photograph, *c.* 1910. The portico and front walls are all that survive of the original 1835 building, designed by the Pains and built by the Deanes. On Good Friday 1891, the Courthouse was destroyed by fire and only the aforementioned portions were allowed stand in the new Courthouse designed by W.H. Hill, which opened in 1895. The sculpture on the pediment, 'Justice, Hibernia and Commerce', is by the Cork-born sculptor Thomas Kirk.

Grand Jury

Cork Courthouse was the venue for the biannual meetings of the County Grand Jury. Its members were the leading landowners in the county and were responsible for county administration insofar as they had the granting of contracts for roads, bridges and other public works. In advance of the first local government elections in 1899, they met for the last time in the Grand Jury Room when this photograph was taken. Twenty-two Grand Jurors sit at the table (one was absent) and four officials stand to the rear. The twelfth juror from the left is the foreman, Sir Arthur Hugh Smith-Barry of Fota.

Queen's Place

Located adjacent to Clarke's Bridge and not far from the Courthouse, Queen's Place, seen in a 1930s Camera Club photograph, was built in the late eighteenth century. A fine terrace of four houses, built for the residential use of the merchant middle class, the houses had by 1901 become tenements occupied by a total of eleven family or individual units. Their decline accelerated to dereliction by the 1960s and they were demolished in the 1970s. The site of Queen's Place is now the car park of the Social Services Centre, which opened in 1990.

Royal procession at the Courthouse
The tiered steps of the Courthouse feature as a grandstand for spectators to view the passing parade of the royal entourage during the 1903 visit to Cork of King Edward VII. 'The progress of the Royal visitors through Great George's Street was marked by a manifestation of a cordial character. Handkerchiefs were waved from the windows of the houses, on the roofs of many of which persons had occupied positions and cheers were raised by a large number of the bystanders. For the entire length of the thoroughfare the decorations were pretty numerous' (*Cork Examiner*). The photograph is from the Newsom collection in Cork City Library.

EXTERIOR OF FACTORY.

Lee Boot Factory

This Guy's photograph taken in 1913 shows the staff of the Lee Boot Factory in sidecars outside their place of employment on Lancaster Quay prior to embarking on their annual excursion. The Lee Boot Manufacturing Co. was established by the Dwyer family around 1880 to complement their wholesale drapery business. Originally located in Hanover Street, it soon moved to larger premises on Washington Street, and about the time this photograph was taken had expanded to take over the old Lancasterian Schools, which were replaced by a new building on the Mardyke.

St Joseph's National School

St Joseph's Monastery N.S., on the Mardyke, photographed here by Guy's in 1914, replaced the Lancasterian Schools on Lancaster Quay. The Lancaster schools in Cork were established in 1812. Rev. John England (later Bishop of Charleston, USA) was associated with the early years of the school, before they were taken over by Bro. Michael Riordan's Presentation Monks in 1827. St Joseph's National School, also conducted by the Presentation Brothers, had twelve classrooms to accommodate 550 children. It was designed by the Cork architect Samuel Hynes and built by Messrs J. Kearns & Sons, Cork.

Mardyke

Lewis's *Topographical Dictionary*, published in 1837, described the Mardyke as 'the principal promenade, a fine raised walk a mile long, extending through the meadows between two branches of the river, and shaded by a double row of lofty flourishing elms ...' By 1893, when this Guy's photograph was published, the Mardyke was said to be 'not now nearly the fashionable rendezvous it was in bygone days'. The century after 1893 was not kind to the Mardyke – the stately elms died, the promenade became a roadway and the 'fashionable rendezvous' was no more.

Exhibition House

At a meeting of the Corporation in February 1901, Lord Mayor Edward Fitzgerald mooted the holding of an International Exhibition in Cork, an idea that came to fruition in May 1902, fuelled by his energy and the organisational skills of several others. Purchasing a house and lands beside the Mardyke Walk called 'The Shrubberies' and leasing adjoining lands, the Exhibition Committee constructed an elaborate complex of buildings to house a wide range of cultural and industrial exhibits, as well as fairground attractions. Among the buildings was the 'portable house' pictured here.

Exhibition – Cormac's Chapel

During its 1902 season (1 May – 1 November), the International Exhibition attracted over one million visitors. The attractions were varied; industrial and machinery halls, a Grand Concert Hall and a Women's Section vied for attention with amusements that included the Great Water Chute and the Switchback Railway. The attention to detail in buildings and exhibits is apparent in this photograph, published in the *Irish Rosary*, which shows the reproduction in fibrous plaster of doorways from Cormac's Chapel at Cashel.

Royal Visit to Exhibition
The success of the 1902 season prompted the Exhibition Committee to reopen again in 1903. The highlight of the 1903 season was the visit to the exhibition grounds on 1 August, during their Irish tour, of King Edward VII and Queen Alexandra. This photograph, possibly taken by a member of the Newsom family, shows the Royal carriage about to depart, at the conclusion of the visit, from the 'Mansion House', as 'The Shrubberies' was called for the occasion. 'The Shrubberies' would in later years become the Cork Public Museum.

St Vincent's from the Grounds
The attractive setting chosen for the 1902–03 Exhibition is illustrated in this 1902 photograph, published in the Dominican magazine the *Irish Rosary*. Electric launches, gondolas and wherries plied on the Lee, where the seventy foot high Great Water Chute was erected. The verdant sloping gardens of Sunday's Well on the other side of the river, as well as the impressive St Vincent's Church and Presbytery (framed by the riverside trees in this view) provided a pleasing backdrop to the Exhibition grounds.

Lord Carbery, aviation pioneer

The highlight of Cork Week in 1914 was an exhibition of flying on 9 July in his Morane-Salinger monoplane by twenty-two-year-old aviation pioneer Lord Carbery. This *Cork Examiner* photograph, shows Carbery (left) and his mechanic posing beside the plane at the Mardyke grounds on 3 July prior to a reconnaissance flight. Following his youthful passion for fast cars and aeroplanes, Lord Carbery had a chequered career. He sold his Castlefreke estate in 1919 and emigrated to Kenya where he was part of the 'Happy Valley' set and acquired a reputation for violent, eccentric behaviour.

Fitzgerald's Park

Following the conclusion of the Exhibition in 1903, most of the buildings were dismantled, but 'The Shrubberies' and grounds were presented to the citizens of Cork as a recreational area. It was decided to name the grounds Fitzgerald's Park in honour of the Exhibition's initiator, who was also honoured by being created a Baronet. Features of the Exhibition Grounds were preserved in the Park, including the Fr Mathew Fountain, seen here in a 1918 Guy's photograph.

Bandstand, Mardyke

A much-loved corner of Cork's Mardyke is depicted in this *Cork Examiner* photograph from the summer of 1939. This was the Band Field with its attractive band stand, for decades a favourite haunt for Cork's brass band enthusiasts (and its water pump, a magnet for young boys on a hot summer day). In 1982 the Band Field and bandstand made way for a two-lane roadway linking Western Road and the Mardyke. Though regular recitals had declined by then, it was regretted by many when this corner of old Cork was sacrificed to traffic flow demands.

Cork Piper's Club

Pictured here in a City Library photo are the members of the Cork Piper's Club. The presence with the group of the Brian Boru figure who featured in the 1914 St Patrick's Day parade suggests 1914 as the date. Founded in March 1898, the survival to maturity of the Piper's Club owed much to the enthusiasm and energy of John Smithwick Wayland until his emigration to Australia in 1912. The club's Republican leanings are suggested by the fact that their bandrooms in Hardwick Street were destroyed by fire in the weeks prior to the Burning of Cork.

National Dramatic and Choral Society

Amateur dramatic and musical societies flourished in Cork in the early decades of the twentieth century. Most notable were the Daniel Corkery-associated Cork Dramatic Society and the Munster Players, but there were many others. Popular venues, besides the Opera House, were St Francis Hall, St Finbarr's West Temperance Hall and Fr Mathew Hall. This photograph from the Cork City Library collection is believed to be the cast of a production of *The Colleen Bawn* by the Cork National Dramatic and Choral Society and is dated to between 1914 and 1920.

Blackpool National Prize Band

The Blackpool National Prize Band pose on the steps of the North Monastery schools in this 1907 photograph. The photographer was A.H. Somerville, who plied his trade from Quaker Road on the other side of the city. Cork's numerous bands had their origins in the temperance movement or were associated with particular occupations or localities. They came out *en masse* for occasions such as St Patrick's Day and nationalist parades. In the early twentieth century, they became increasingly associated with the factionalism of O'Brienite and Redmondite politics.

Burning of the Opera House

On the night of 12 December 1955, Cork Opera House was destroyed by fire; this *Cork Examiner* photograph shows passers-by inspecting the ruins the following morning. Its origin had been as the main hall of the 1852 Cork National Exhibition and had been reconstructed on this site in 1855 as the Athenaeum. It was altered and enlarged in 1877 and reopened as the Theatre Royal and Opera House. In 1888 it became the Cork Opera House under new management. Cork had no major theatre for a decade until the opening of the Michael Scott-designed new Opera House on this site in 1965.

Crawford Municipal Technical Institute

This Guy's photograph, *c.* 1918, depicts the Crawford Municipal Technical Institute in Sharman Crawford Street. Formally opened on 16 January 1912, this building gathered under one roof the burgeoning range of science and technical classes offered by Cork Corporation's Technical Instruction Committee. An initial difficulty with its provision was solved by A.F. Sharman Crawford's offer of a free site on Fitton Street, formerly occupied by Arnott's Brewery. The street and school were renamed in his honour. The 'Tech' was vacated in the late 1970s when Cork RTC was built; in 1979 it became the new home of the Crawford School of Art.

St Finbarre's Cathedral, c. 1862

The Church that preceded the modern St Finbarre's Cathedral occupied an early medieval monastic site and, incorporating portions of an earlier church, was built in 1725–35. This photograph, presented to Cork City Library by Alec R. Day in 1939, shows the tower and steeple of the eighteenth-century cathedral, prior to its demolition in 1865. To defray the expense of its building, a duty of one shilling per ton was imposed by act on all coal and culm imported into Cork for five years from 1 May 1736.

Crawford Municipal School of Art

This Guy's photograph, c. 1910, is of the Crawford Municipal School of Art in Nelson (now Emmet) Place. This incorporated the old Custom House (to the right of the turret), built in 1724, which later housed the Royal Cork Institution from 1832 to 1849, in which latter year it was reopened – as a Government School of Design. In 1884 a large extension, designed by Arthur Hill, was harmoniously added. Its principal benefactor was W.H. Crawford; hence the name it has borne since. It served as both art school and gallery until 1979 when the School transferred to Sharman Crawford Street. Since then it has prospered as the Crawford Municipal Art Gallery.

Tower and Chancel, 1864

Following a decision in 1862 to replace the old St Finbarre's with a more imposing edifice, the old cathedral building was dismantled in 1865. A unique photographic record of the dismantling was made by the amateur photographer Thomas R. Lane; a collection of nine views, annotated by Richard Caulfield, was published in 1866. This photograph from Lane's collection was reproduced by Rev. Andrew Robinson in his 1897 guidebook and shows the tower and, behind it, the chancel exposed by the partial dismantlement of the building.

West front of St Finbarre's

The west front of St Finbarre's, built of Ballinasloe limestone, is the most notable feature of the exterior and especially its three recessed portals, featured in this Guy's photograph. The three portals are ornamented with statues of the Apostles, of the Wise and Foolish Virgins and of the Bridegroom, the central figure. The tympanum over the middle portal represents the Resurrection. A restoration and development programme for St Finbarre's Cathedral was launched in 2000.

Burges's St Finbarre's Cathedral
The architectural competition for designs for the new St Finbarre's Cathedral, announced in 1862, was won by the English architect William Burges. His French Gothic design was not without its detractors as it had ignored the stated budget of £15,000 and indeed had a final cost of £100,000. The foundation stone was laid in 1865 and the cathedral was consecrated in 1870. The magnificence of Burges's Cathedral with its soaring spires is captured in this photograph taken from the eastern end of Bishop Street by G.M. Roche, *c.* 1905.

UCC Quadrangle

University College, Cork, or as it was originally known, Queen's College, Cork, was opened for the reception of students in 1849. Designed by Sir Thomas Deane, it earned from the historian and essayist Lord Macaulay the compliment of being 'a Gothic College worthy to stand in High Street of Oxford'. The original buildings, seen here in a Guy's photograph, *c.* 1910, occupy three sides of a quadrangle opening to the south. The western range of buildings, which originally contained laboratories, was destroyed by fire in 1862 and rebuilt shortly afterwards.

Dairy Science Building, UCC

William T. Cosgrave, President of the Executive Council, lays the foundation stone for the Dairy Science Building, UCC, on 20 July 1928 in this *Cork Examiner* photograph. This development was seen as an important contribution to rural Ireland's economic future and was also linked to the past glories of Cork's provision trade. The ceremony, which took place in sweltering heat, was attended by delegates to the World's Dairy Congress as well as by the usual dignitaries. W.T. Cosgrave's Cork connection is often forgotten; despite his Dublin background, most of his parliamentary career was spent as a TD for Cork Borough (1927–44).

La Retraite

Photographed here, around 1940, is La Retraite, a hall of residence for women students of UCC, which was opened in October 1923, and was run by the La Retraite sisters, a French order. Situated to the west of Gaol Walk, it had originally been Lee Cottage, the residence of the gaol governor and later of the Murphy-O'Connor family. Following enlargement in 1967, it could accommodate ninety students. In 1977 the buildings were acquired for college activities by UCC and La Retraite hostel moved to College Road. Renamed Áras na Laoí, they were greatly extended in 1991.

St Bonaventure's

St Bonaventure's, a hostel for Capuchin students attending UCC, is the subject of this photograph, *c.* 1940. Located at Victoria Cross, the property had a varied history. For over sixty years, it was Victoria Lodge, the residence and nursery of the Haycroft family, seed merchants and nurserymen, until its purchase, *c.* 1910, by the Cudmore family. Acquired by the Capuchins in 1917, it was extended several times before its purchase and conversion to a hotel *c.* 1990, when it was again extended. In 2002, most of the complex was demolished with the exception of the building on the left, prior to the development of multi-storey student apartments.

Munster Institute

The Munster Institute on Model Farm Road (to which it gives name) was originally the Munster Model Farm School, founded in 1853 by the Board of National Education as one of a number of model farms for teaching agriculture. Its original purpose was not realised and in 1880 it was reconstituted as the Munster Dairy School and Agricultural Institute, specialising in the dairy industry. Its brief expanded later to include poultry management and up to its closure in 1984, it trained students in poultry-keeping and farm home management. The photograph of the main building is by Guy's and was published in 1919.

Victoria Station

This photograph from the 1890s shows Victoria Cross, then at the western extremity of the city. Here was located the first outward-bound station on the Cork & Muskerry Light Railway; an inward-bound train can be seen in the photograph. The last toll-house in the western suburbs, conducted by the Irwin family, survived here until 1925. The building in the centre of the photograph, then Long's public house, has changed hands, but is still a popular hostelry. However, the scene today is transformed by the presence, a few hundred yards beyond the public house, of the fourteen-storey Cork County Hall, built in 1968.

Cork Motor Race, 1936

From 1936 to 1938 international motor racing came to Cork with annual motor races on the Carrigrohane circuit. The series culminated with the 1938 Cork Grand Prix. This photograph shows Prince Bira of Siam in his 1936 entry, the 1488 cc. ERA. Bira was one of the more colourful drivers and participated each year, though he failed to finish in the 1936 and 1937 races. In 1938, Bira finished second in the Grand Prix and won the Light Car Race. A genuine Siamese prince, Bira was born in Bangkok in 1914 and died in London in 1985.

Road Surfacing Works

Roadworks were not invented by some evil genius in the late twentieth century. This photograph, reproduced from a Corporation report, shows resurfacing in progress on an unidentified street in 1914. The Trinidad Lake Asphalt Paving Co. were contractors for a major road surfacing programme that began in 1912. To provide crushed stone to underlay the asphalt paving, they established a plant on Albert Quay using stone from a quarry at Killeady. Managing director of the company was Maurice Talbot Crosbie, who unsuccessfully contested Cork City in the 1918 election.

Roadworks at Lower Glanmire Road

This photograph also records the Corporation's 1912–14 programme of roadworks, although the scene here could have occurred any time up to the 1960s, when steamrollers and horse and cart were still in use for roadworking. The location under repair here is the stretch of Lower Glanmire Road between St Patrick's Church and the Railway Station. The type of resurfacing being laid here was called Durax Pavement. In the background is St Patrick's Terrace.

Wharf construction

This 1912 photograph is of wharf construction on the south side of the river between the Deep Water Quay and the Marina. This wharf was constructed using reinforced or ferro-concrete, a relatively new concept; in 1907 the building of a reinforced concrete bridge at Mizen Head in West Cork had been a pioneering works. The workmen in the foreground are mixing concrete, which will be poured into moulds and, while still moist, will have reinforcing iron strips imbedded in it.

Resurfacing Patrick Street

Wood block paving was extensively used in surfacing the city's principal streets. Two of the main streets were thus paved in the 1880s and in 1912–14 three-quarters of a mile of street embracing 16,500 square yards were repaved in wood. This *Cork Examiner* photograph shows the wood block paving being taken up in Patrick Street in July 1932. The wooden blocks or setts are being salvaged by children to take home for use as firewood.

Accident on Sullivan's Quay

This photograph from the *Cork Examiner* archives records the result of a now unusual collision, between a motor car and a horse-drawn vehicle. On 1 July 1939 the car, having struck a horse and cart at South Gate Bridge, went out of control, mounted the footpath at Sullivan's Quay, in the process injuring a woman pedestrian, before crossing the road and crashing into the iron railings on the quay side. Fortunately the upper bar and stone pillar prevented the car crashing into the river at full tide. The occupants, four young men and two children, escaped serious injury.

Train/Steamroller collision

This *Cork Examiner* photograph depicts the most unusual traffic accident in Cork's history. It occurred on 6 September 1927 on the Carrigrohane Road. A train of the Cork & Muskerry Light Railway was travelling towards Cork on the roadside track when a steamroller engaged on road repairs ran into it causing the derailment of two coaches. Perhaps because it was a relatively slow speed impact, there were no serious injuries and, strangely enough, the steamroller fared badly, its front roller becoming dislodged.

Patrick Street, 1872
In this photograph we see the Patrick Street of the 1870s; it can be dated to the years 1872–74, when a horse tram service operated in the city, one of which trams is seen in the foreground. On the right of the photograph is Carmichael's drapery store, which would later become Cash & Co. On the skyline in the centre of the photograph is the Scott residence in Sidney Place that would in 1885 become Government House, the residence of the general officer commanding the Cork Military district. To the left below it was the Vincentian Schools building in St Patrick's Place, later the Christian Brothers College.

Brian Boru Street in the 1930s
This 1930s *Cork Examiner* photograph of Brian Boru Street evokes a sense of wonder at the apparent ease with which several dozen pigs are being herded towards the bridge. Their destination was probably Murphy's bacon factory on Evergreen Road. Brian Boru Street was created in 1911–12 as part of the City Link Railway development; the railway cutting on the right still exists though it last saw a train in April 1976. The small lock-up shop on the right also survives, but has been unoccupied in recent years. The building on the left was a postal sorting office until about 1990.

Patrick Street, with white horse

In this Guy's photograph of Patrick Street in the early 1900s, there is a great deal of activity both on the street and on the pavement, suggesting that perhaps the photo could have been taken in 1902 or 1903 during the Cork Exhibition. While the white horse in the foreground catches the eye, there are in fact a dozen horse-drawn vehicles in view as well as two trams. The premises on the right, which include Cash & Co., would be among those that bore the brunt of the destructive Burning of Cork in 1920.

Patrick Street, c. 1905

This postcard view of Patrick Street dates from 1900–05. In the right foreground are examples of pre-tram transportation, the covered car and the side car. There were seven car stands in Patrick Street. On the extreme right is Day's saddlery premises. Further to the left is the entrance to Bowling Green Street. The pedimented doorway to the left of the street entrance was the entrance to Wesley Chapel, built in 1805, when this part of Patrick Street was still called Colvill's Quay.

Patrick Street, London House
This Raphael Tuck postcard view, *c.* 1900–02, of Patrick Street shows on the right Atkins' London House drapery store. The three women on the right appear to be mother and daughters, dressed, like almost everybody in view, in black but with summery white head wear. The occupants of the carriage and pair of horses seem to be military. The advertisement board on the Blackrock tram heralds a method of transport then coming into vogue – the bicycle; the advertiser was R.B. Baker of King Street, agent for several makes of cycle.

Patrick Street, Newsom's shop
This photograph, *c.* 1910, is of Patrick Street at its junction with French Church Street (on the left) and Marlboro Street (on the right). On the extreme right is the long-established grocery business of Newsom & Sons. The Newsoms were one of Cork's prominent Quaker business families. Incidentally, in 1913, the employees of Newsom's had one of the leading inter-firm hurling teams in the city. Further to the left can be seen the porticoed entrance to the Royal Victoria Hotel, originally known as the Chamber of Commerce Hotel from its association with that body.

Patrick Street/Fireman's Hut

This Stewart & Woolf postcard view, *c.* 1900, shows a rather deserted Patrick Street. The lack of activity allows for a good view of a structure that has a long association with the street – the fireman's hut behind the Fr Mathew statue. This was built in the early 1890s to provide shelter for a fireman in charge of the heavy rescue ladder, which can also be seen in picture. The ladder became obsolete in 1930 with the advent of ladder-equipped fire engines and the hut was taken over by the city bus service, the Statue being an important bus terminus. The hut was removed in 2002 as part of the regeneration of Patrick Street

Recruiting office

Mangan's Clock, seen in this 1915 *Cork Examiner* photograph, is as familiar a part of Patrick Street as the Father Mathew statue. The clock has survived, though the premises that gave it birth, James Mangan Ltd, at 3 Patrick Street was demolished in the construction of the Merchant's Quay complex. During the First World War, No. 2, Patrick Street was an army recruiting office. In this photograph, a military band is performing outside the office. During World War 1, 11,569 men enlisted in the Cork Recruiting Area; several thousand others were already in the army or enlisted elsewhere.

Three young women

The Victoria Hotel features in the background of this late 1950s photograph of three young women walking along Patrick Street. It is probable that these young women are on their way home from work, but they recall the popular Cork pastime of 'doing Pana'. This simply entailed walking up and down Patrick Street (the 'Pana' of the expression), seeing and being seen. This innocent weekend pursuit, in a city that still considered itself a community, evaporated in the age of motorised transport and consumerism.

Royal procession in Patrick Street, 1903

This photograph from the Alec R. Day collection at Cork City Library shows the Royal Carriage preceded by a mounted escort passing along Patrick Street on 1 August 1903 at the culmination of the visit to Cork of King Edward VII. This was part of the route to Glanmire Railway Station following the royal visit to the Exhibition at the Mardyke. The background streetscape shows the Munster Arcade, Egan's and Forrest's, which would all be destroyed in the 1920 fires. On the far side of Cook Street from Forrest's is seen the Royal Victoria Hotel.

95–96 Patrick Street
The front door of 95 Patrick Street, home of a Cork institution, the *Cork Examiner*, features in this 1931 *Examiner* photograph. Founded in 1841 by John Francis Maguire, the *Examiner* is the Republic's oldest newspaper. The neighbouring London and Newcastle Tea Co. were at No. 94 for over seventy-five years; their name survived as the L & N supermarket chain. The shabby façade of 1931 was being remedied at No. 96 (O'Flynn's Butchers) by workmen from the firm of Barrett & Sons.

Waiting for news, 1940
This *Examiner* photograph was taken on 10 May 1940 when crowds waited anxiously outside the newspaper office for the appearance of the *Evening Echo* with news of the German invasion of the Low Countries. CNN or the Internet were a long way off in 1940! The upper floors of 94–96 Patrick Street were later extensively renovated incorporating a pedimented central bay of windows over the *Examiner* office door. In the early 1990s the *Examiner* abandoned its Patrick Street entrance for an entrance on Academy Street and changed its name to the *Irish Examiner* in 2000.

Patrick Street, c. 1940

This aerial view of Patrick Street, *c.*1940, shows a marked contrast to earlier views. The tram system had departed almost a decade earlier and the motor car has firmly established its presence, although most of the cars here appear to be taxis. In the distance a bus rounds the curve of the street at Burton's. Patrick Street is the least straight of the city's principal streets and curves in a shallow semi-circle from the Bridge to Grand Parade. The curve reflects the course of the waterway that it once was.

Patrick Street, Burton's/Grant's

An eerily deserted Patrick Street, photographed in the early morning presumably, is seen in this 1960 photograph. Though the street frontage has not changed dramatically in the last forty years, some prominent businesses, familiar names to generations of Corkonians, have since departed the scene. The building in centre view was from 1927 to the 1980s, Burton's, the menswear shop, while the large building to its right was Grant's department store, a business established in the 1840s by Sir John Arnott. On the right, the vertical sign for the Pavilion recalls one of the city's popular cinemas, which closed in 1987.

Merchant's Quay

Merchant's Quay, showing a distinct lack of uniformity in its streetscape, is profiled above the balustrade of Patrick's Bridge in this 1960 photograph. In the nineteenth century, Merchant's Quay had a very maritime tone, its business premises including ship brokers and agents, as well as the Cork Sailor's Home. This gradually changed after the building of Brian Boru Bridge. The tall plain building to the left in this photograph was the St Vincent de Paul Hostel, built *c.* 1950 due to the efforts of Charles K. Murphy.

Merchant's Quay/Patrick Street

A Cork street corner that has disappeared is recorded in this 1960 photograph of the corner of Merchant's Quay and Patrick Street. An interesting feature of the corner building, rebuilt in 1931 as the Cork Gas Consumer's Company showrooms, was the tower on its roof which had on its visible faces plaques showing the city coat of arms and was surmounted by a glazed gas-lit lamp. The buildings in the foreground were demolished in 1987 during the development of the Merchant's Quay shopping complex, the largest reconstruction project that the city had experienced since the rebuilding following the 1920 fires.

St Patrick's Bridge, 1890

St Patrick's Bridge is featured in this early 1890s Guy's photograph. The first bridge here was opened in 1789 at a time when Patrick Street was being created and was originally a toll bridge, with a portcullis to allow shipping through. That bridge was destroyed in a great flood in 1853. A temporary wooden bridge spanned the river until the new St Patrick's Bridge was opened in 1861. John Arnott laid the foundation stone in 1859; he was created a baronet on that occasion and was Sir John when he opened it.

Tram on Patrick's Bridge

This postcard view, *c.* 1910, of a tram at the southern end of Patrick's Bridge provides a fine vista of the north side of the river. In the background are Pope's Quay and Camden Quay, and profiled against the skyline are the tower of the Dominican Priory and the steeple of St Anne Shandon. Alcocks, the grocers and tea merchants, advertised on the tram, had a grocery business at 74–75 Patrick Street and had warehouses at Brown Street.

Patrick's Bridge, east side

St Patrick's Bridge is attractively profiled in this Guy's photograph, *c.* 1910, taken from an elevated position on Merchant's Quay. Though the photograph shows a large number of pedestrians, it conveys a more leisured atmosphere than would be found in the frenetic activity of a modern street scene. In 1910 there was time to lean on the parapet of the bridge or to stop and read the advertising boards. The building on the extreme right on St Patrick's Quay housed the Tara Refreshment Saloon, which operated here for almost fifty years.

Camden Place

Camden Place, prominently featured as backdrop to St Patrick's Bridge in this early 1900s postcard, derives its name from the Earl of Camden, Lord Lieutenant for Ireland in 1795. This terrace was built from the proceeds of a successful Tontine speculation around 1800 and the development was popularly known as the 'Tontiles' at one time. For much of the nineteenth century, it was almost totally occupied by the city's medical elite, though by the early 1900s the Edinburgh Temperance Hotel had been established there and by the 1920s, there were three hotels in Camden Place.

Cyclist

A lot of water has flowed under the bridge since a cyclist so enjoyed the freedom of the highway as Denis Healy does in this late 1940s photograph taken on St Patrick's Bridge. In the background, 10 Bridge Street, at this time long established as a bank branch, is surrounded by scaffolding. In the 1950s, before the motor car became a household object, the bicycle was a popular mode of transport and the change of shifts in factories such as Ford's and Dunlop's was marked by an armada of cyclists making their way to and from work.

St Patrick's Quay, 1960

St Patrick's Quay, in this 1960 photograph, exhibits a variegated streetscape displaying a mixture of architectural styles. The seed merchants, John Atkins & Co. Ltd, occupied 3–5 St Patrick's Quay in 1960, premises that a century earlier had been the warehouses of Burke's, corn merchants and Hackett's, tanners. The attractive gabled façade of No. 5 with its triple-arched ground floor has a not untypical Cork mixture of red sandstone with limestone dressings. It is now occupied by the Victoria Sporting Club leisure centre.

French Church Street

French Church Street, off Patrick's Street, is seen in this Camera Club photograph in the 1930s. The building in the left foreground is identified with the Huguenot Church that gives its name to the street. The Huguenots of Cork, who contributed greatly to eighteenth-century Cork, worshipped in a church on the site from 1712 to 1813. It was later used by the Primitive Wesleyan Methodists (1819–97), but the original church was pulled down and replaced by a Methodist Chapel in 1845. A small Huguenot graveyard survives here behind the streetscape. Later occupants of the building were Newsom's and the Cork Radio and Electrical Trading Co.

From the Statue to the top of the hill

What could be dubbed 'the Patrician Way' is revealed in this 1930s Camera Club photograph taken from a Patrick Street rooftop. The foreground shows the Fr Mathew Statue and beyond that St Patrick's Bridge, Bridge Street and St Patrick's Hill disappear into the distance. The steep incline of St Patrick's Hill has frequently been selected over the past century to test man and machine. It has seen reliability tests of motorcycles, motor cars and trucks and has featured in the Cork stages of both amateur and professional cycle races.

Quaker Meeting House
Cork's Quaker community has made an enormous contribution to the city's social and commercial life over the centuries. This photograph by Cork Camera Club is of the Quaker Meeting House in Grattan Street and dates from the late 1930s. The first Friends' Meeting-house in Cork was built on this site in 1677 and was taken down and rebuilt in 1777. It was rebuilt again in 1833 at a cost of £3,338, George Beale being the architect-builder. In 1937, the building, unsuited for the community's declining numbers, was sold to the Cork Board of Public Assistance for use as a dispensary and the Cork Society of Friends moved to a new, smaller meeting-house at Summerhill South.

Old Post Office façade

This 1870s photograph shows the façade of the old Post Office in Pembroke Street. Originally built in 1824 for the Cork Savings Bank, it was vacated by them in 1842 and was let to the Cork Small Loan Fund until its demise in 1857. It was then leased to the Postmaster-General for a Post Office. It was incorporated into the new General Post Office in the late 1870s and this façade appears to have survived until *c.* 1902 when it was taken down.

Post Office Staff, 1933

The staff of Cork's General Post Office posed for this group photograph in 1933. By then, the official address of the GPO was Oliver Plunkett Street, having been around the corner at Pembroke Street up to a few years previously. The postal service at the GPO in 1933, as recorded in Guy's Directory, was comprehensive. The hours of business were from 8 a.m. to 7 p.m. from Monday to Saturday and the office was even open briefly on Sundays, Christmas Day and bank holidays. The postmaster was John Twomey.

Telephone cabling at Winthrop Street, 1927

It was probably a novelty to see a street dug up in 1927 when this photograph was taken; little did the workmen pictured here realise that they were pioneers of an activity that became a national pastime for a while at the end of the century! The location here was Winthrop Street, when a major ducting and cabling scheme for the telephone service was instituted. At the time the telephone exchange was at 91B South Mall and had not yet transferred to the GPO, which is in the background of this photograph.

The Old City Hall

The old City Hall, seen here in a Guy's photograph about 1910, was originally the Cornmarket or Corn Exchange, built in 1833 and greatly enlarged for the 1852 Cork Industrial Exhibition. It also housed the 1883 Cork Exhibition and in 1889 was acquired by the Corporation and converted to use as the Municipal Buildings. A Town Hall was added in 1906 at a cost of £5,300, primarily to house the 1902–03 Exhibition organ which had been presented to the Corporation provided that a suitable building be erected to house it. It was from that date that the term City Hall was accorded to the building.

The New City Hall

Following the City Hall's destruction in 1920, the Corporation opted to defer construction of a new City Hall and to apply the compensation received to the pressing matter of housing. After the re-establishment of the City Council in 1929, it was decided to rebuild on the old site. The new City Hall, seen here in a 1940s postcard view, was formally opened in 1936. Designed by Messrs Jones and Kelly and built by Sisks, it consisted of two wings housing the Municipal Offices with an Assembly Hall between. The façade is of Little Island Limestone.

Formal opening of City Hall

The honour of laying the foundation stone for the new City Hall in July 1932, and of formally opening it on 8 September 1936, fell to Éamon de Valera in his capacity as President of the Executive Council. Some of the formality of the latter occasion is captured by this photograph of the landau bearing de Valera and the Lord Mayor, Ald. Seán French, to the City Hall. They were attended by a mounted escort of honour, clad in blue and gold uniforms and wearing black bearskin hats.

Missionary Exhibition
City Hall had already been partially occupied prior to its official opening in 1936 and hosted
a Missionary Exhibition in 1934. The model of a pagoda promoting the Maynooth Mission
to China in this photograph is believed to be part of that exhibition. This mission society
had strong Cork associations, being co-founded in 1916 by Co. Cork-born Fr (later Bishop)
Edward Galvin. The two workmen posing beside the elaborate model, one of whom is
identified as carpenter Denis Healy, were responsible for its construction.

Anglesea Bridge/Parnell Place

Warren's Place (later renamed Parnell Place) and the bank buildings that flank its entrance, the Provincial Bank on the left, the Cork Savings Bank on the right, are seen in this early 1880s photograph. In the right foreground is Anglesea Bridge, built in 1830, which was replaced in 1882; the new bridge was named Parnell Bridge. Anglesea Bridge had a centre lifting arch to allow shipping through. Cork Savings Bank, regarded as one of Cork's finest buildings, was designed by Thomas and Kearns Deane and opened for business in August 1842.

Morrison's Quay/South Mall Corner

This photograph, *c.* 1890, shows the junction of Morrison's Quay and the South Mall. The premises seen here with a horse and cart at its entrance was owned by A. Sutton & Son, coal merchants. Around 1900, Suttons consolidated the buildings at this end of the South Mall into an office and business premises called Sutton's Buildings (not to be confused with the housing development of the same name on the Old Youghal Road). Sutton's was destroyed by fire in 1958 and was replaced by a modern office block.

Provincial Bank, South Mall

This Guy's photograph, *c.* 1918, might be mistaken for an elaborate wedding cake, were it not for the figures posed on the pavement outside. It is the Provincial Bank at the corner of South Mall and Parnell Place built in 1866 to the design of the Dublin architect William G. Murray. Despite its ornate style as seen here, it fits well into the South Mall street-scape. Photographs do not in fact do justice to the elaborate sculptural detailing.

Munster & Leinster Bank

The Munster & Leinster Bank, 63-66 South Mall, is the subject of this Guy's photograph, *c.* 1918. Built between 1911 and 1914 to the design of Arthur Hill, the building work was undertaken by John Sisk & Sons, Cork. The building occupies a site where the Union Bank originally stood. This was succeeded by the Munster Bank, which was forced to cease trading in 1885, but was rescued through the efforts of James J. Murphy who was instrumental in establishing the Munster & Leinster Bank. The bank is now the Cork head office of Allied Irish Banks.

Commercial Buildings

This Guy's photograph, *c.* 1900, shows the Commercial Buildings, incorporating the Imperial Hotel, on the South Mall at its junction with Pembroke Street. The Cork Commercial Buildings Co. was incorporated by royal charter in 1808 and commissioned the building, which was completed by Sir Thomas Deane in 1813. In 1816 they resolved to erect a hotel at the rear, also built by Deane, which became the Imperial Hotel and in the course of time outgrew its parent company, its main entrance moving from Pembroke Street to the South Mall frontage.

Chamber of Commerce

For almost 75 years Cork had two competing Chambers of Commerce. When the original Chamber, founded in 1818, elected Parnell as its President in1881, business interests in the city felt that the Chamber was being politicised and in 1883, they formed the rival Cork Incorporated Chamber of Commerce and Shipping. This photograph of their Council in 1918 is from *Cork: its trade and commerce*, their official handbook, published in1919. Included are several of the city's largest employers. In the centre of the front row are James Dwyer (Vice-President) and A.R. Mc Mullen (President).

South Mall

The western end of South Mall, *c.* 1870, is seen in this photograph from the Alec R. Day collection in Cork City Library. The attractive bow-fronted houses that formed the southern end of the Mall and that were subsequently demolished were then occupied by Alexander McCarthy, solicitor and Town Clerk, and by the medical practice of Dr Wall. The building at the corner of Grand Parade, No. 45, was occupied by J. Green, engravers.

LDF Parade

The military parade in this photograph was the largest of its kind in the history of the state. It took place on 13 September 1942 at the end of a military exercise in the Cork area in which the regular army and volunteer forces participated. The photograph shows Éamon de Valera reviewing the parade in South Mall. Major MacDonnell leads the Local Defence Force (LDF); the LDF officers include C.J.F. MacCarthy (first from left), later a noted local historian and Anthony Barry (fifth from left), later a Lord Mayor. They are followed by the 47th Battalion, LDF, led by Commander Brett. The photograph was presented to Cork City Library by C.J.F. MacCarthy.

South Channel, Parliament Bridge

'The pleasant waters of the River Lee' are depicted in this postcard view of the South Channel, *c.* 1940. To replicate this view today the photographer could stand on Nano Nagle Bridge, a pedestrian bridge built in 1985 to link Grand Parade and Sullivan's Quay. The bridge seen here is Parliament Bridge, one of the city's older bridges, designed by William Hargrave and opened in 1806. Beyond it the graceful spire of Fr Mathew's Holy Trinity Church soars skyward.

South Chapel

The earliest extant Catholic church in Cork city is St Finbarr's (South), popularly known as the South Chapel. The site in Dunbar Street (then the Red Abbey Marsh) was acquired by the Dominican parish priest Fr Albert O'Brien in 1766, during the episcopacy of John Butler. Architecturally, the South Chapel is a plain Georgian building, but is artistically distinguished by John Hogan's fine carving in white marble of the 'Dead Christ'. The photograph dates from the late 1920s.

Holy Trinity Church

Cork's Capuchin community, of which Fr Mathew was a member, was originally located at Blackamoor Lane, where their first chapel was built. When that became inadequate for their needs, Fr Mathew selected a site on Charlotte (now Fr Mathew) Quay for a new church and friary. The foundation stone of Holy Trinity Church was laid on 10 October 1832. Work on the G.R. Pain-designed building was hampered by site difficulties and lack of funds. The unfinished church was consecrated on 10 October 1850, Fr Mathew's birthday. This photograph, *c.* 1870, shows the unfinished structure with a simple belfry in place of the lofty spire planned by Pain. Note the amount of shipping that then came this far up the South Channel.

Holy Trinity Church (2)

This photograph, *c.* 1918, takes the same vantage point as the previous photograph, but almost half a century later. In the interim a friary, designed by Robert Walker, was built beside the church in the late 1880s. In 1890, the centenary of Fr Mathew's birth, a competition was announced for the completion of the church. Dominic Coakley's successful design reduced the scale of Pain's original plan; the spire and façade were added in 1891.

MacSwiney funeral
1920 was undoubtedly Cork's *annus horribilis*. The murder of Lord Mayor Tomás MacCurtain was followed by the death on hunger strike of his successor Terence MacSwiney and in December there was the burning of Cork by the Black and Tans. MacSwiney had played a leading role in the formation of the Cork Volunteers in 1913. Arrested at City Hall on 12 August and later sentenced to two years imprisonment, he commenced a hunger strike that ended with his death on 24 October, the seventy-fourth day of his fast. This photograph shows the MacSwiney funeral making its way along the quays.

Patrick Street, 1920

This photograph shows Patrick Street from Cash's to the Munster Arcade in October 1920, two months prior to the destruction of this area. Note that all the premises have shutters or hoardings protecting their plate glass frontage. In the photograph a group of people are being held at the mouth of Robert Street by police and military for searching and questioning during a Sunday afternoon swoop on the city centre. The photographic studio of Brooke Hughes over 27–28 Patrick Street is prominently advertised.

The burning of Cork — Sunner's chemists

The destruction wrought by the burning of Cork on the night of 11–12 December 1920 is reminiscent of the effect of aerial bombardment during World War 2. This photograph shows the surviving façade of R. Sunner's, chemists, 31 Patrick Street. The focal point of the arson attacks in Patrick Street was the section from Merchant Street to Cook Street in which every premises was destroyed. In the weeks prior to 11–12 December, a number of arson attacks on city business premises had presaged the events of that night.

The burning of Cork – the morning after

The ruins of Patrick Street on the morning after the burning are seen in this photograph. Firemen are still damping down the smouldering ruins. There is considerable evidence that the efforts of the Fire Service to control the fires were thwarted by some of the Black and Tans. The section pictured here was occupied by Roches Stores and several other businesses. The buildings to the left — the Patrick's Bridge side — mark the extremity of the destruction in that direction.

City Hall after the fire

Arson attempts on the City Hall in October and November 1920 resulted in little more than superficial damage. On Sunday morning, 12 December, the arsonists were successful. According to a fireman's testimony, 'about 2.45 am, (we) saw .two men carrying petrol tins coming from Union Quay. (They) went into City Hall. After 4.30 am we heard a man shout, "stand clear", and an explosion occurred in the City Hall; this was followed by ten or twelve intermittent explosions'. This photograph shows the façade of the City Hall on the following morning.

City Hall interior

This photograph is of the interior of part of the City Hall following the fire. The degree of destruction is indicative of the use of explosives as suggested in the evidence of firemen rather than the effect of fire only. In a preposterous attempt at damage-limitation, Sir Hamar Greenwood, Chief Secretary, stated in the House of Commons that the City Hall and adjoining Library were set alight by sparks from the Patrick Street conflagration.

Frankfort, Montenotte

The destruction of property in the city that began in 1920 continued intermittently through 1921–22 when the perpetrators were more often the IRA targeting police or military installations and the residences of persons deemed overly sympathetic to the Crown. In May 1921, Frankfort, Montenotte, seen here in a 1910 photograph, was burned by the IRA. Frankfort was the residence of Sir Alfred Dobbin, a prominent city businessman, who was High Sheriff in 1900. His wife, Lady Kate Dobbin, was a noted Cork artist in later years. After the fire they lived in the Imperial Hotel, of which Sir Alfred was a director.

Business resumes in Patrick Street
In the aftermath of the Cork burnings, the first task was the clearing of rubble and debris from the devastated sector of Patrick Street. By early January 1921, businesses whose premises had been destroyed were beginning to re-establish a presence on their former sites. This photograph from early January shows in the foreground a hut in which Egan's, the jewellers, displayed a small portion of stock; beyond it is the Munster Arcade inquiry office, the first temporary building to be completed. Faintly discernible in the right background is the Lee Cinema.

Crowds view the ruins
The flames that engulfed the city centre late on Saturday 11 December and on Sunday morning were visible citywide and the accompanying volleys of gunfire that punctuated the night left few in any doubt of the seriousness of the occurrence. It was not until Sunday morning and afternoon, however, that citizens ventured out in large numbers to view the devastation. In this photograph, stunned Corkonians in Patrick Street view the wreckage of a familiar streetscape.

Egan's, Jewellers
The rebuilding of Patrick Street after the 1920 fires gave the city some of its finest business premises. Cork's leading architects and builders were involved in the design and construction of fine buildings such as Roches Stores, Cash's and Egan's. One of the first to rise phoenix-like from the ashes was the premises of William Egan & Sons at 32–33 Patrick Street. This 1924 photograph shows that building starkly outlined by the absence of adjacent buildings. A long-established firm and the city's leading firm of silversmiths and manufacturing jewellers, Egan's ceased trading in 1990.

Carnegie Library

This postcard view, *c.* 1910, shows Parnell Bridge with the Town Hall and City Library in the background. The library, on Anglesea Street, was one of the first Carnegie Libraries in Ireland. In 1902 Andrew Carnegie offered a £1,000 grant to Cork Corporation to build a library. Plans prepared under the direction of Henry A. Cutler, City Surveyor, were approved and in October 1903 Carnegie accepted an invitation to visit Cork to lay the foundation stone. During his visit, he was made a Freeman of the City. The library was opened on 12 September 1905 by the Lord Mayor, Ald. Joseph Barrett.

Carnegie Library in ruins

Cork's Carnegie Library was to have a short life. It was one of the buildings destroyed on the night of 11-12 December 1920 by the Black and Tans; its destruction was probably a consequence of its nearness to City Hall. This photograph from the *Report of the Labour Commission to Ireland* shows the façade of the library after the fire; the interior of the building and its contents were destroyed. For some years following 1920, the city was without a public library until a temporary premises was acquired in Tuckey Street in 1924.

Ald Cors Buckley

'All politics is local politics', according to some pundits and this was very much the case in Cork in the years prior to World War I, when the rival nationalist factions, the 'Molly Maguires' and the 'O'Brienites', supporters of John Redmond and William O'Brien respectively, gave an intensity to local politics that boiled over at election times. This 1914 photograph shows Ald Cors Buckley (left) being congratulated by Hugh Martin, the United Irish League organiser, on Buckley's victory over an O'Brien candidate in the North-West Ward Corporation election. Buckley, a vintner from Church Street, died in 1915.

Collins at St Francis' Church

On Sunday, 12 March 1922, Michael Collins, Chairman of the Provisional Government, addressed a Pro-Treaty meeting on Grand Parade, attended by an estimated 50,000 people. Despite some interruptions and revolver shots being fired in the air, the meeting was very successful. That morning, Collins and his party attended Mass at St Francis' Church and were formally welcomed by members of the Community in the monastery garden where this *Cork Examiner* photograph was taken. From left to right, Diarmuid Fawsitt, Commdt Garret Cooney, Fr Louis, OFM, Michael Collins, Pádraig O'Keefe TD, Frs Leo and Edmund, OFM and Commdt Seán McKeown.

Collins' Funeral
Michael Collins's death in an ambush at Béal na mBláth occurred on Tuesday evening, 22 August 1922. Overnight, the corpse of the dead Commander-in-Chief of the National Army was laid out in Shanakiel Hospital, the casualty station for wounded Provisional Government forces. On Wednesday afternoon, the Collins funeral cortege set off through the suburbs and city streets to Penrose Quay, whence the remains were carried by sea to Dublin on board the *SS Classic*. This *Cork Examiner* photograph, taken at Gaol Cross, Western Road, shows the funeral procession headed by Cronin and Desmond's hearse bearing the tricolour-draped coffin.

Cork Typographical Society

Founded in 1806 with an initial membership of twenty-eight, the Cork Typographical Society was still flourishing in 1906, when it was decided to form a Centenary Committee to celebrate the Society's one hundred years. One of the committee's achievements was the publication of a handsome Centenary Souvenir from which this photograph is taken. Chairman of the committee was W. Baillie, who occupies the 'chair' in the photograph.

Workers at Morrogh's

Loom room employees at Morrogh's Woollen Mills at Donnybrook, Douglas in 1933 are pictured in this *Cork Examiner* photograph. Morrogh's Mills, established in 1889, were in mill premises formerly occupied by Wallis & Pollock's Flax Spinning Mill. By 1903, they employed 300 people, many of whom were housed in the 100 company-owned cottages in Douglas; in 1933, the workforce was 150. The original enterprise was financed by John Morrogh, who had made his fortune in the Kimberly Diamond mines, becoming a director of De Beers. He was a Nationalist MP for Cork SE, 1889–93.

Metropole Buildings

Metropole Buildings, the focus of this early twentieth-century photograph, were developed by the Musgrave brothers to the design of Arthur Hill and built in 1896–97 by the building firm of John Delaney & Co. The development incorporated a hotel, a sweet factory (to the rear) and shop units. At the time this photograph was taken, the shops were occupied by Correll's drapers, one of Musgrave's own shops and to the right of the hotel entrance, Lawson's, a very old Cork firm of gent's outfitters and hosiers. Hadji Bey's, the confectioners, were later a prominent tenant.

King Street

King Street, seen here in a postcard view in 1902, had been known as Strand Road in the late eighteenth century. It was renamed again in the early 1920s, when it became MacCurtain Street in commemoration of Lord Mayor Tomás MacCurtain, murdered by Black and Tans in 1920. For much of the nineteenth century, the street was noted for Paul McSwiney's King Street Iron Works, but in the late nineteenth century there was extensive upmarket commercial development of the eastern end of the street.

Trinity Presbyterian Church

Trinity Presbyterian Church, at the foot of Summerhill, photographed in the 1890s, is an attractive and distinctive church, not least because of its crooked spire. Designed by the London architect John Tarring, it opened for worship in July 1861. Its congregation numbered several of the prominent Scottish merchants who were influential in Cork business in the nineteenth century. One of their number, John Carmichael, was the benefactor of the Carmichael Schools (to the left of the Church), also designed by Tarring and built by Robert Walker. The foundation stone of the school, which closed in the 1960s, was laid on 5 August 1863.

Metropole wedding reception

The MacMahon wedding party feature in this early 1950s photograph. The photograph was taken at the Metropole Hotel in the popular location for wedding group photos at the hotel — on the roof! The other unusual aspect of Metropole wedding receptions was that the hotel did not have a drinks licence; the original Musgrave brothers — strict Methodists — were anti-drink. The hotel allowed wedding parties to hire in a bar and charged a modest corkage fee, a system that ended in 1956, when the hotel obtained a drinks licence.

St Luke's Church

St Luke's Church (Church of Ireland) was not long rebuilt when this Guy's photograph was taken, around 1890. The original church on this site, purchased in 1834 for £40 from Thomas Johnson, a shipbroker, was consecrated in 1837; it was re-built and enlarged in 1875, but was destroyed by fire in February 1887. It was immediately re-built to the design of W.H. Hill and re-opened for Divine Service in 1889.

Military Party on Summerhill

The military presence in Cork was a significant social and economic factor in the city and evoked little resentment among the general populace prior to the War of Independence. The military participated at various civic occasions and regimental bands regularly provided musical entertainment at public events. This photograph from the City Library collection is of the Leinster Regiment on Summerhill returning to barracks having attended Mass at St Patrick's Church on St Patrick's Day 1913.

St Patrick's Church

Prominently featured in this postcard view of Lower Glanmire Road is St Patrick's Church. Built in 1836 as a chapel of ease to the North Cathedral, it became a parish church in 1848. Associated with its establishment was Rev. Fr Francis Mahony ('Fr Prout'), who subscribed £100 to the building fund, but disagreed with Bishop Murphy on where it should be sited. Mahony had abandoned the priesthood for a literary career before it was built. The Celtic Cross in the lower right was an advertisement for the nearby monumental works of John A. O'Connell.

Tram at Summerhill

From December 1898 to September 1931, Cork city had an electric tram public transport system. The Father Mathew statue was the hub of the system from whence lines radiated to termini at Blackpool, Summerhill, Tivoli, Blackrock, Douglas and Sunday's Well. There were three through cross-city routes: Blackpool — Douglas, Summerhill — Sunday's Well, Tivoli — Blackrock. This Alec R. Day photograph features a tram at the Summerhill terminus at St Luke's Cross in the early years of the century. In the background is Rockspring Terrace.

Hardwick Street

A quiet corner of Cork city in the mid-1930s is recorded in this Camera Club photograph of
the lower portion of Hardwick Street and the northern end of Pine Street. Hardwick Street is
a connecting street between St Patrick's Hill and Leitrim Street/Coburg Street; it was here that
the Piper's Club had their bandroom. The business premises in picture are at the northern end
of Pine Street and were Hoskins' public house, Coughlan's hardware store and O'Riordan's
shop.

General view of Northside

This postcard view of Cork's Northside includes three of the area's most notable landmarks. The churches on the skyline are St Anne Shandon on the left and the North Cathedral on the right. The photograph is dominated however by the 200ft chimney stack of Murphy's Lady's Well Brewery on Leitrim Street. Established in 1865 in the grounds of the former Foundling Hospital, Murphy's quickly became Cork's largest brewery. The chimney stack survived as a prominent landmark until 1985 when it was taken down for safety reasons.

Corpus Christi, Madden's Buildings

This amateur photograph, taken in the 1930s, shows Madden's Buildings decked out for the annual Corpus Christi procession. Madden's Buildings, located between Great William O'Brien Street and Watercourse Road in Blackpool, was Cork city's first municipal housing scheme. The development of seventy-six single-storey houses was undertaken on what had been the Blackpool Market site and was completed in 1886. The houses were three-roomed dwellings costing £85.10.0. each. They had no front garden, but had a backyard and were built of red brick.

Great William O'Brien Street, 1930s

This is probably a Sunday afternoon scene in the 1930s. A group of adults and children sit or stand outside a shop on Great William O'Brien Street, adjacent to its junction with Water Lane. A motorcycle and sidecar are the object of curiosity on the part of the adults; of admiration, perhaps, on the children's part. Great William O'Brien Street had formerly been called Great Britain Street, before being renamed in honour of the Mallow-born parliamentarian. Water Lane (now Seminary Road) was the birthplace of James Barry (1741–1806), the noted Irish artist.

Blackpool Tram

The Blackpool tram features in this interesting photograph taken at Blackpool in 1922–23. Included are five soldiers in Free State uniform, presumably part of the force that took over control of the city in August 1922 in the course of the Civil War. Note the two passengers on the upper deck, which was open to the elements. The seated capacity of a tram was 45; 25 on the upper deck and 20 downstairs. The indicator board (DS) on this tram signified Douglas — Statue, Douglas being the terminus at the other end of the Blackpool route.

O'Leary's, Pine Street

The side car of jarvey Packie (Slasher) Murphy is seen here outside the undertaking establishment of Dominick O'Leary in Pine Street. It will be noted that O'Leary also advertised cars and carriages for hire; this was not unusual and indeed several undertaking firms became involved in the motor trade when that type of 'car' came into vogue. O'Leary's went out of business here around 1909, dating the photograph to the early years of the twentieth century.

The Rock Steps

When Cork expanded beyond the walled city of the sixteenth century, settlement crept up the hillsides to the north and to the south of 'the flat of the city'. To the south, the slope is moderate, but on the northside, it is much steeper. A consequence of this are the numerous steps that link river-side developments beside the north bank of the Lee with developments higher up. The Rock Steps, linking the North Mall with Blarney Street, are one example. This photograph, c. 1960, shows a group of happy youngsters posing on the Rock Steps.

Outside Eustace's

The horse waits patiently, while the news of the day is exchanged. A scene more reminiscent of rural Ireland than a city centre side street, this 1930s Camera Club photograph is of Devonshire Street North, looking towards Coburg Street. The horse and cart are at the entrance to Eustace's, the builder's providers, 'suppliers of every requisite for any building from foundation to roof'. By 1925, when the Dinan family had a controlling interest, the firm were also proprietors of the Shandon Candle Works.

Keyser's Lane

The southside, less steeply inclined, has fewer steps than the northern hillsides. An exception is Keyser's Lane or Hill, which wends its way from French's Quay, past Elizabeth Fort, towards Barrack Street. This 1930s Camera Club photograph shows the small houses that follow the lane up the hill. The word 'keyser' is of Scandinavian origin, meaning 'the passage leading to the waterfront'. The occurrence of the name has been adduced as evidence of Ostmen influence in this area in the distant past.

Unidentified steps

The unidentified passageway in this photograph from the years before the First World War was probably quite pleasant, even charming, in midsummer, but horrendous in the winter months when rainwater cascaded down the steps. This passageway did have the advantage of public lighting and was of reasonable width. The young boy posing at the foot of the steps and the two smaller children beside him are apparently well dressed.

Sanitary arrangements, city tenement

The sanitary facilities at a city tenement are depicted in this 1910 photograph. Fr M. McSwiney described the conditions and facilities at a Cork tenement around this time: 'There is a small yard, about ten feet by six, with one water closet and one water tap which do duty for the whole house. Each house has at least four families and some of them are larger than average. In one of these tenements there were seven families occupying eight rooms.'

Northside Lane, early 1900s

This photograph of an unidentified northside lane dates from the early years of the twentieth century. Though such lanes of small dwelling houses still survive in the city, there are obvious differences. The gable-ends are whitewashed, but unplastered, the laneway is roughly cobbled and the paint scheme of the houses on the left lacks modern sublety. The women at the mouth of the lane date the photograph more firmly than any other feature; they could indeed appear in a photograph of a North African townscape.

City tenement

Tenement life was perhaps even grimmer than life in the narrow lanes, where there was a greater community spirit. This photograph, dated around 1910, of a Cork tenement was published in a study of social conditions in Cork. Describing a visit to a tenement, Fr M. McSwiney wrote: 'There were seven families occupying eight rooms. In another I found a family of thirteen persons — a father, mother and eleven children aged between four and seventeen – all living in two rooms and a hole called a kitchen.'

Children in a laneway

Several children pose for the photographer with a mixture of curiosity and indifference in this study of a Cork laneway around 1910. Even in the early twentieth century, a significant proportion of the city's population lived in overcrowded conditions in narrow lanes and alleys such as this one. Life was not necessarily unhappy in such conditions, but by modern standards it was certainly grim, claustrophobic and conducive to poor health. The little lad to the left, holding something more like a cricket bat than a hurley, is more likely to have hurled than played cricket.

Cornmarket Street

Cork's open-air market at Cornmarket Street, long known as the Coal Quay, was still a vibrant produce market when this Camera Club photograph was taken in the 1930s. Part of the essential Cork for many who remember it in its heyday, it was not without its detractors at times. 'Cornmarket Street is made a refuse ground for all the vegetable waste of the vendors who use it for this purpose', reported the City Engineer in 1915. The limestone façade in the background dates from the eighteenth century and is part of the original Cornmarket, which is credited to an Italian architect, Allesandro Galileo.

The Doll's House

The Dutch-style Queen Anne house in this 1930s Camera Club photograph was popularly believed to be the oldest dwelling house in the city. Located on Bachelor's Quay, it was officially known as the 'Sheriff's House', but in later times, having become a tenement house, it acquired the name the 'Doll's House', under which name it featured in Frank O'Connor's 1932 novel, *The Saint and Mary Kate*. By 1961 it had fallen into decay, its tenants vacated it and it was boarded up. A few years later, in 1966, the 'Doll's House' was demolished.

Good Shepherd Convent
The Convent of the Good Shepherd in Sunday's Well, seen here in a postcard view, *c.* 1910, was built in 1870–71. Designed by G.C. Ashlin and built by O'Flynn's of Watercourse Road, its establishment owed much to the generous patronage of James Hegarty of Sunday's Well. It comprised three departments, a convent, an Industrial School and a Magdalen Asylum (originally called St Finn Barre's New Magdalen Asylum) for the reform of prostitutes or 'penitents'. A recent architectural historian has remarked on its echoes of Lhasa's architecture, but for many of its inmates there was little Buddhist peace.

The Bridewell

This decorative building resembling a Lego-brick construction, familiar as background in photographs of the Coal Quay Market, was the Bridewell at the northern end of Cornmarket Street, a site now occupied by the Bridewell Garda station. The Bridewell was used for the temporary confinement of prisoners before final committal and of disorderly persons taken up in the night until brought before the magistrates. In August 1922, as the National Army captured Cork, the Bridewell was among a number of buildings burned or blown up by the retreating Republican forces.

Daly's Bridge

Cork's only suspension bridge, and its most charming, is seen here as the location for a family photograph in the late 1950s. Daly's Bridge, known colloquially as the 'Shakey Bridge', spans the Lee from Sunday's Well to the southern bank, where a ferry boat had operated until the 1900s. It owes its existence to the generosity of city businessman James Daly, who paid half the cost of the bridge. Spanning 160 feet, it was officially opened in April 1927 and was built to the design of S.W. Farrington, City Engineer.

North Mall

At one time the most fashionable place of residence in Cork was the North Mall, photographed *c.* 1939 by the Cork Camera Club from the entrance to the North Mall Distillery. At the beginning of the nineteenth century it was the city's most fashionable promenade and in 1867 the occupants of its elegant town houses included Robert Jennings, John Lane and Francis Wise, all prominent merchants. The Wises were proprietors in the nineteenth century of the distillery and their name survives in Wise's Hill. The building at the extreme left at the foot of Wise's Hill was a bonded warehouse.

No. 8 North Mall
The fanlighted Georgian doorway of No. 8 North Mall is the subject of this 1930s photographic study by the Cork Camera Club. Formerly the residence of Francis Wise, the distiller, it was in the 1930s the home of Michael Holland. Holland, antiquarian, topographical artist and illustrator, was a life-long member of the Cork Historical and Archaeological Society, and for a number of years contributed a weekly illustrated strip to the *Cork Examiner* called 'This quaint old Cork of ours'. He died, advanced in years, in November 1950.

North Gate Bridge

This postcard view, published in the Emerald Series, shows the North Gate Bridge and the bottom of Shandon Street in the early 1900s. The bridge seen here was opened on St Patrick's Day 1864 and had been built in eleven months. Designed by Sir John Benson, the building contractor was Barry Mc Mullen; the clerk of works was Jerome J. Collins, a young Corkman, later a noted meteorologist and a member of the ill-fated *Jeannette* expedition to the Arctic.

Girls at North Gate Bridge

Three little girls in summer dresses pose for a family photograph in the late 1950s. They are standing beside a pillar of the old North Gate Bridge on the southern bank of the north channel. The North Main Street/Bachelor's Quay street-scsape that they are facing has changed entirely in the intervening years, but the scene behind them showing part of Newsom's Quay and the bottom of Shandon Street remains much as it was over forty years ago.

Dunscombe Fountain

This photograph dates from the early 1930s and is from the Cork Camera Club collection. It shows the square at the foot of Shandon Street, a locality popularly known as Goulnaspurra. The beshawled women are gathered around Dunscombe's Fountain, functioning at this point as a gas lamp standard rather than a fountain. It was removed in May 1935. In the background is the pawnbroking premises of W. Jones. The pawnbroker's symbol, three brass balls, can be seen to the right of the downpipe. The building to the right of Jones's was burned in 1920 when it housed Shandon Street Sinn Féin Club.

St Mary's, Pope's Quay

St Mary's Dominican Church on Pope's Quay, seen in this 1902 photograph published in the *Irish Rosary*, was designed free of charge for the Dominicans by Kearns Deane. The foundation stone was laid in 1832 and the first phase of building was completed in 1839. The fine Ionic portico and triangular pediment surmounted by a statue of Our Lady was not added until 1861, when interior alterations were also made.

Vacant lot at North Main Street

Unusually, the focus of this Cork Camera Club photograph of the north-eastern corner of North Main Street is a vacant lot. The empty lot at 2–4 North Main Street was recorded as 'vacant' by Cork directories from 1918 through 1946. This photograph was probably taken in the mid-1930s; the bakery and confectionery on the right was occupied up to the mid-decade by Gerald Darcy. This end of North Main Street at its junction with the quays has been totally redeveloped in recent years and Nos. 1–6 have disappeared, subsumed by a major commercial development.

Bob and Joan

The gateway featured in this 1930s Camera Club photograph was the entrance to the Greencoat School, a charity school established rear St Anne's Shandon in 1716 to educate twenty boys and twenty girls of the parish. Their clothing was green and yellow, hence the name. The two lead figures on the entrance piers, remembered in rhyme as 'Billy Budds and Mary Heafy/Made of lead, and very heavy', were more commonly known as 'Bob and Joan'. The school was demolished in the 1960s but the figures are preserved in the tower of the church.

St Anne Shandon
St Anne Shandon, seen here in an 1892 Guy's photograph, is, like Fr Mathew's Statue and the Mardyke, an emotional landmark for Corkonians home and abroad. Built in 1722, it is distinguished and rendered highly visible by its tower and steeple, the latter surmounted by a golden weathervane in the form of a salmon. The tower has two limestone faces and two in red sandstone, hence its 'pepper-pot' nickname. Its clock, installed by James Mangan in 1847, has four faces, which do not always tell the same time, hence the witticism, 'the four-faced liar'. The famous Shandon bells, immortalised by Fr Prout's verse, were set up in 1750.

North Cathedral

This 1950s postcard view of the North Cathedral, taken from some distance up Cathedral Road, provides an interesting counterpoint to the photographs of Bailey's Lane. The wide roadway seen here had been the densely populated laneways of a generation earlier. The North Cathedral, or St Mary's and St Anne's to give its formal name, had been rebuilt in 1820 after it had been extensively damaged by fire. The tower and western door were added in the 1860s. The Cathedral was extensively refurbished in the 1990s.

Clearance area south of Bailey's Lane

This photograph was taken in 1933, probably from the tower of St Mary's Cathedral and shows the huddle of houses and narrow lanes south-west of the Cathedral. The lane in the lower right was Bailey's Lane, which ran westward from the Cathedral. Much of the area in the foreground was cleared in the 1930s redevelopment of this part of the city. The early stages of development of the Gurranebraher housing scheme – Cork's 'red-roofed city' – can be seen in the distance on the right. Designed by J.R. Boyd Barrett, the first phase of the scheme was blessed by Bishop Cohalan on 17 March 1934.

Bailey's Lane

This 1932 photograph from the same vantage point as the previous photograph shows in closer detail the Bailey's Lane area. In the lower left is the corner premises on Shandon Street, then occupied by Walsh's pharmacy and O'Callaghan's grocery. At the near end of Bailey's Lane was St Mary's Temperance Hall and Cinema. From the narrowness of the lane and congestion of the area, one can gauge the lack of natural light and ventilation. Bailey's Lane and the adjacent property were demolished subsequently and later became the modern Cathedral Road.

Eucharistic Procession

Popular religious devotion was measured by the throngs who participated in the city's annual Eucharistic Procession. Cork's first Eucharistic Procession took place on 6 June 1926; the original suggestion for the Procession is reputed to have come from Professor C.K. Murphy. This *Examiner* photograph shows the culmination of the procession — Benediction from an altar erected at the National Monument — on 26 May 1940. A reported 40,000 took part in the procession. In later years the altar was constructed at Daunt's Square at the other end of Grand Parade.

Funeral of Bishop Cohalan

The funeral of Bishop Daniel Cohalan was the occasion for this *Cork Examiner* photograph of parishioners gathered at the corner of Shandon Street and Cathedral Road across the road from the Cathedral in August 1952. Despite the solemnity of the occasion, it will be noted that most were conscious of the camera; the roadsweeeper, however, stood to attention like an old soldier. Bishop Cohalan, born in 1858, in Kilmichael, Co. Cork, became Bishop of Cork in 1916 and after a thirty-six-year episcopate, died on 24 August 1952, aged ninety-four.

North Monastery

In 1818, seven years after arriving in Cork, the Christian Brothers opened the school at Our Lady's Mount that would become the famed North Monastery. A period of expansion was begun in 1898–99 with the erection of the Gerald Griffin Memorial Technical School, which was enlarged in 1903 when building of the adjacent Brother Burke Memorial School commenced; funds for building the latter were raised as a tribute to Bro. Burke on the occasion of his Golden Jubilee. Additional storeys were added to both schools in 1911–13. The 1918 Guy's photograph shows the Griffin Technical School on the left, the Burke Memorial School on the right.

Christian Brothers Cemetery

In the little cemetery of the Christian Brothers' monastery at Our Lady's Mount, seen in this Guy's photograph, *c.* 1892, are buried the deceased members of the community. Among those resting in the community cemetery are Gerald Griffin, the novelist and poet, author of *The Collegians*, briefly a member of the community before his untimely death in 1840 and Bro. James Dominic Burke, the most notable of the Order's educationalists in Cork and a pioneer of technical and science education, who died in 1904.

Pageant

To celebrate the centenary of the Christian Brothers in Cork, an Irish historical pageant was staged over three days in September 1911. The pageant, scripted by Bro. Walker and directed by Joseph Curtis, was based on the Red Branch cycle of tales and was held in the grounds of the monastery. A cast of 500 pupils participated in the performance. This photograph from the Cork City Library archive shows one group of Celtic warriors performing at the pageant.

Christian Brothers College

In 1888, with the opening of the new Diocesan College at Farranferris, the Christian Brothers assumed control and direction of the former St Finbarr's Seminary at St Patrick's Place, off St Patrick's Hill, and it was renamed Christian Brothers College. The Seminary originated in the old Mansion House under the Vincentians, before transferring to the former Everton Schools in St Patrick's Place under Diocesan management. The new school, photographed here c. 1930, was a great success; together with their great rugby rivals, Presentation Brothers College, they provided secondary education aimed at the middle-classes. Vacated in 1988, it is now the headquarters of 96FM radio station.

Cork — Senior Hurling Champions 1928

To paraphrase Bill Shankly, hurling was not a matter of life and death in Cork city in times past; it was much more than that. Intense inter-club rivalry existed at local level, but was put aside (usually) when the players donned the red and white. The 1928 Cork All-Ireland senior hurling winning team, pictured here, includes many of the players who brought the championship Leeside in 1926, 1928, 1929 and 1931. Included are Jim O'Regan, Seán Óg Murphy and Jim Hurley, Eudie Coughlan and the Aherne brothers, all household names in their day.

Cork hurlers
This Cork hurling group photograph is undated, but is probably contemporaneous with the previous picture. Included in the photograph are Seán Óg Murphy (*centre, front row*), later Secretary, Cork County Board, for many years; Sean McCarthy (*right, front row*), Chairman Cork County Board 1917–37 and President of the GAA 1932–35, later a TD and four times Lord Mayor; Jim Hurley (*left, middle row*) served as Meath County Manager 1942–43 and as Secretary/Bursar, UCC, 1944–65. Jim Barry (*centre, middle row*) was for many years associated with Cork teams in a training capacity.

Ring and Seberg

The late Seán Beecher in his *Story of Cork* tells a Christy Ring story, illustrative of Cork wit, of which the punchline is: 'Who's dat in de picture with Ringey?' This *Cork Examiner* photograph was taken at the Athletic Grounds on 27 September 1959 after Glen Rovers had edged out UCC in the County hurling semi-final. The maestro, who had a quiet game punctuated by two decisive, match-turning passes, is shaking hands with Jean Seberg, the film actress, who was in Cork promoting *The Mouse that Roared* at the Film Festival. Both were, sadly, to die prematurely; Ring in March 1979 aged fifty-nine and Seberg, six months later, aged forty-one.

Lynch leads Glen Rovers

This *Examiner* photograph features another of Cork's best-loved sons. Jack Lynch, destined to lead his country, leads his Glen Rovers team-mates in the parade before their County senior hurling final against Sarsfields at the Athletic Grounds on 29 September 1940. For the record, the Glen won their seventh successive title on a remarkable scoreline of 10-6 to 7-5, Glen corner-forward Charlie Tobin scoring six goals. Jack Lynch's leadership qualities were early recognised by GAA officials; he first captained the Cork senior hurling team in 1938 at the age of twenty-one.

Blackrock Tennis Tournament

The favoured sport of Cork's upper middle class in the early twentieth century was lawn tennis and this photograph by Brooke Hughes, which was published in the society magazine *Irish Life*, shows a group of competitors at the Blackrock Lawn Tennis tournament in July 1913. Blackrock won the Munster Lawn Tennis Cup on the eve of the tournament and were a leading tennis club. The Daly and Haughton families provided their leading players. James Daly, 'one of the best tennis players we have in the south', won the Gent's Singles at the tournament, which ran for several days.

Blackrock Castle

Picturesque Blackrock Castle, seen in this early 1900s photograph by Roche of Dublin, is at once Cork city's most famous castle and not really the genuine article. Though its site has been fortified since about 1582, the earlier structure was destroyed by fire in 1827 and was replaced by the modern structure in 1828–29, built to the design of James and G.R. Pain. From the seventeenth century, the Mayors of Cork held an Admiralty Court at the Castle, from which devolved the triennial custom of 'Throwing the Dart', followed by a banquet at Blackrock Castle. It was used as a hotel and restaurant from the 1960s, but is now unused.

Throwing the Dart

This photograph records the ancient ceremony of 'Throwing the Dart' being performed by the Lord Mayor, Ald Henry O'Shea on 21 July 1914. The ceremony, performed triennially at the time, was enacted by the Chief Magistrate of the City to mark the municipal jurisdiction over the Port of Cork. The Lord Mayor and 550 guests on board the *SS Ardmore* dined well before reaching the harbour's mouth where he cast a golden-headed javelin into the sea as a symbol of his authority. The occasion, it can be observed, was a male-dominated one and historically appears to have been an enjoyable day out for the boys.

Blackrock Hurling Club

Blackrock, besides having a fishing tradition and a picturesque castle, has been famous since the foundation of the GAA as a hurling stronghold. Blackrock National Hurling Club, called Cork Nationals until 1888, dominated Cork hurling up to 1931, during which period the club won twenty County senior titles and provided six All-Ireland winning Cork team captains. This photograph from the City Library collection is of an early 1920s Rockies team and includes county stars such as Seán Óg Murphy, Paddy Aherne, Paddy Delea and the Coughlan and O'Connell brothers.

THE MARINA, CORK

The Marina

'Let's all go down the Marina' ran a local ditty attesting to the popularity of the Marina Walk. Construction of the Marina, so named in 1780, began in 1763 with the building of a navigation wall along the south shore of the river towards Blackrock, to prevent the channel from being choked with mud. The area behind the wall was gradually reclaimed by depositing mud from the channel. The made land became a popular promenade and recreation area. This 1930s postcard view looks westward along the Marina towards the city. Across the river can be seen the lower slopes of Montenotte.

The Marina (2)
The popularity of the Marina promenade resulted in additional amenities being provided, such as the bandstand seen here in an Emerald postcard view around 1905. A double row of elms planted by Prof. Murphy of Queen's College as a growing experiment in 1856 greatly added to the recreational ambience. Another Marina landmark was the Flagstaff, a 140-foot Douglas fir presented to the city by Capt Hanson of the *Grainger* in 1864, which stood on the Marina until it had to be cut down for safety reasons in 1935.

The Marina (3)
The pleasures of the Marina were greatly enhanced by its commanding view of the river and of the verdant tree-lined hills of Montenotte on the further shore. This Guy's photograph, *c.* 1892, taken from beside Shandon Boat Club on the Marina, shows the Montenotte and Tivoli hillsides with Carrig House, Bellevue Terrace and Woodhill Terrace on the riverside. These residences are actually separated from the river by a roadway and the Cork-Cóbh-Youghal railway and were accessed by railway pedestrian bridges, two of which can be seen in this photograph.

Cork Regatta

The Marina provided a natural grandstand for one of the city's big annual events, the Cork City Regatta. On Regatta day, huge crowds thronged both the Marina and the northern shore to see Ireland's premier rowing crews battle for such coveted prizes as the Leander Cup. This photograph from the Cork City Library collection shows the finale of one of the regatta events in 1911. The buildings in the background are Myrtle Hill Terrace (left), Bellevue Lodge beside it and Carrig House on the right.

Cork Park Racecourse

Cork Park Racecourse at the Marina, seen here in a 1916 Guy's photograph, was for forty-seven years one of Ireland's most popular racecourses. From 1869 to 1902 it was leased to Sir John Arnott and from 1902 to the Arnott-controlled Cork Racecourse Ltd. In 1913 a new lease at annual rent of £175 was granted to Cork Park Racecourse Ltd. A condition of this lease was that if the Park was required for the purpose of a factory, it could be taken by the Corporation without compensation on giving three months notice, a clause that was invoked in 1916 to allow Fords purchase it for their factory.

Excavating the Ford site
The Easter race meeting in 1917 was the last held at Cork Park racecourse and soon after work commenced on the Ford factory site. A large workforce was employed on excavation of the site, which proved more expensive to develop than anticipated as it required much levelling and pile-driving. The wharves, foundry and machine shop were built first. By summer of 1919 it was ready to begin production and the first tractor left the assembly line on 3 July 1919. This photograph from the Ford archive is of excavation work in progress on 12 November 1917.

Bird's eye view of the river

This bird's eye view of the river east of Custom House around 1918 shows the Ford factory on the Marina at an early stage of development. Beyond it can be seen the as yet undeveloped expanses of Cork Park. This photograph, taken from the heights of Montenotte, also shows, from left to right on the northern bank, the Harbour Commissioners' yard, the former Cork Steam Packet Co.'s dockyard and the railway yards of Glanmire Station. On Lower Penrose Quay can be seen the masts of sailing ships and steamships.

The Marina in the 1950s

The industrialisation of the city end of the Marina had reached its peak when this photograph, from a similar vantage point to the previous view, was taken in the 1950s. The area, in addition to Ford's car assembly plant, now also hosted the Marina Generating Station, Dunlop's and other manufacturing plants. In its heyday the area had a workforce of over 3,000, though numbers had declined to about 1,500 when Dunlop's closed in 1983, followed in 1984 by the closure after almost seventy years of the Ford plant.

Ships at Patrick's Quay
This postcard view of the North Channel and St Patrick's Quay predates 1912 when Brian Boru Bridge was opened, providing the first bridge on this channel down-river of St Patrick's Bridge. On the left can be seen the rear of the Palace Theatre (its entrance was on MacCurtain Street) which had opened on Easter Monday 1897 as 'Dan Lowrey's Palace Theatre of Varieties'. Having had a period of decline, it reopened in December 1959 and had its third coming as the Everyman Palace Theatre in 1990.

The Quays, Cork

Penrose Quay, the hub of Cork's cross-channel ferry services for almost 150 years, is the subject of this postcard view from the early 1900s. The building on the right, designed by the Pains, was built in 1832 as the offices of the St George Steam Packet Co.; hence the sculpture on the pediment of St George killing the dragon. The company was reorganised in 1843 as the City of Cork Steam Packet Co., which in turn was absorbed by the Coast Lines Group in 1918 and became a subsidiary of the B & I Group in 1936.

Disembarking passengers
This busy quayside scene depicted in a Guy's photograph around 1900 shows passengers disembarking from a cross-channel steamer. In 1898, three sailings per week operated from Cork to Milford Haven and to London, two sailings to Bristol and to Glasgow and one sailing a week to Cardiff and Newport. A variety of horse-drawn vehicles await the passengers. Hackney carriage fares within the borough boundary were fixed and an average fare would have been a shilling.

Mayflower *at Merchant's Quay*

This photograph, of indeterminate date, but *c.* 1920, shows the steam tug *Mayflower* at Merchant's Quay. The *Mayflower* was one of several vessels owned by Palmers of Ringaskiddy, who provided tug and ferry services in Cork Harbour from the late 1890s. The master of the *Mayflower*, Capt Harrison, is standing by the mast; those in picture include Mrs Harrison and several of her sisters. In the background is St Patrick's Quay, with the Metropole Hotel on the extreme left. The photographer, an employee of Palmers, was the creator of the Lewis/Palmer collection.

Mayflower *at Lapp's Quay*

Another photograph from the Lewis/Palmer collection, this again shows the *Mayflower* around 1920, in this instance embarking passengers at Lapp's Quay for a harbour pleasure trip. Harbour boat trips were a popular Sunday outing. The late Charlie Nash of Cóbh described such an outing: 'A day on the *Green of Aghada*, wasn't it wonderful. Dancing, games, fruit and currant bats. The Dad in the pub, even the band can't get him out. But then the band starts an old favourite, "Hurray, me boys, we're Homeward Bound".'

PS Albert *en route to Crosshaven*

The furthest reaches of Cork Harbour were made accessible to ordinary Corkonians by the vessels of the Cork, Blackrock and Passage Railway Co., known as the 'Green Boats'. From 1850 to 1925, the CBPR operated a steamer service in conjunction with its trains. This photograph, *c.* 1908, is of the *PS Albert* in Cork Harbour en route to Crosshaven. The *Albert*, built in Belfast in 1881 for the company, remained in service until 1925. She was scrapped in 1927.

MV Innisfallen *and* **Glengariff**

This 1957 photograph shows the *MV Innisfallen* at her berth at Penrose Quay, with, in the background, the *SS Glengariff*. Penrose Quay was the traditional passenger ship terminal from the 1820s until 1968 when the terminal made its first move downriver (to Tivoli). The *Innisfallen* was almost a synonym for cross-channel travel; the ship pictured was the third of five *Innisfallens* and operated on the Cork-Fishguard route from 1949 to 1967. Indeed, 'Travel the *Innisfallen* Way' was a popular advertising slogan of the City of Cork SP Co. and its successor, the B & I Line. The *Glengariff* was the last vessel to operate a passenger service from Cork to Liverpool (1956–63).

Building Clontarf Bridge

With the opening on 1 January 1912 of Brian Boru and Clontarf Bridges, the Cork Link Railway came into being, linking the GS & WR terminus at Lower Glanmire Road, the Bandon Railway terminus at Albert Quay and railway sidings on the quays. This photograph shows Clontarf Bridge under construction in 1911. Spanning the South Channel from Lapp's Quay to Albert Quay, it was 197 feet wide with a sixty-two foot opening span for shipping. The superstructure on the left housed the engine room to control the lifting mechanism.

Clontarf Bridge in operation
In this 1928 *Cork Examiner* photograph, the lifting span of Clontarf Bridge is seen in operation to allow a cargo boat move up the South Channel. Brian Boru bridge also incorporated a lifting span and the opening of either bridge to allow shipping through halted all rail and other traffic on the bridge; imagine the traffic mayhem that would ensue nowadays! The facility to allow shipping through continued until the early 1950s, but the rail line did not cease operation until 1976.

Custom House

An oblique view of the front of the Custom House is seen in this 1930s Camera Club photograph. Designed by Abraham Hargrave and completed by his son William, the Custom House, located on Lapp's Island, was built in 1814–18. In 1914, Cork Harbour Commissioners took a 999-year lease on the offices. The royal arms on the tympanum was replaced in 1957 by Marshall C. Hutson's carving of the Cork Arms with the appropriate motto *Statio Bene Fida Carinis*, which translates as 'a safe anchorage for ships'.

Men in chimney-pot hats

Among several photographs presented to Cork City Library in 1939 by Alec R. Day was this early Cork photograph, which is captioned: 'SW Corner of Custom House showing men in chimney-pot hats standing on quay, *c.* 1861'. To our modern eye, the figures in the photograph appear stiff and immobile, almost like waxwork figures, but it must have required some cajoling on the part of the unidentified photographer to persuade his eight 'models' to pose for the required photograph.

Custom House sheds

From a vantage point at Marina Mills, this 1930s Camera Club photograph focuses on the eastern end of Custom House Quays and encompasses a vista stretching away to the north and west of the city. The buildings to the rear of the Custom House offices include bonded warehouses and sheds. The vessel berthed at Penrose Quay is probably one of the cross-channel ferries in operation during the 1930s, the second *Innisfallen* and the *Kenmare*.

Horse-drawn tram at Victoria Road

Horse-drawn trams provided a public transport service for a brief period (1872–75) in Cork city and this photograph from that period shows one of the six trams at the junction of Victoria Road and Victoria Quay where the service had a terminus. The trams linked the railway terminuses north and south of the river as well as serving the city centre. Disagreement between the operators of the system and the Corporation hastened its demise. The London Clown Cricketers advertised on this car were a touring novelty cricket team.

Furlong's Marina Mills

This photograph, published in a Guy & Co. publication in 1919, shows John Furlong's Marina Mills. The Marina Mills, completed in 1891, were located on Victoria Quay, and were the first custom-built roller mills in the city to take advantage of the new deep-water berthage. (Furlongs also operated mills at Lapp's Quay.) The mills, consisting of two four-storey wings with a seventy-eight foot central tower/engine house, were designed by the Cork architect James McMullen. The Marina Mills were demolished in 1986.

Grain Silos on the Marina
The towering milling and grain buildings on the Marina are a familiar sight to those entering Cork along Horgan's Quay. These facilities were built on land leased from the Ford company from 1933 onwards, and were constructed by Cork Milling Co. and National Flour Mills Ltd., companies formed by mergers of several milling concerns.

Lindville Asylum

Lindville Asylum, a private hospital for the mentally ill, designed by Cork architect William Atkins, was opened in 1855 and replaced the establishment founded by Dr T.C. Osburne in 1828 at his Blackrock Road residence, Lindville House. Attractively sited in a fourteen-acre demesne, its proprietor, when this photograph was published in 1911, was Dr C.A.P. Osburne, grandson of the founder. The hospital was demolished in the late 1990s to make way for a housing development. Lindville House, the Osburne residence, is still in existence.

Bridge Street traffic, c. 1930

This photograph, dated around 1930, was taken from a vantage point on St Patrick's Hill and shows Bridge Street, Patrick's Bridge and in the distance, Patrick Street on a sunny afternoon. Though there is considerable pedestrian traffic, there is scarcely any vehicular traffic. Possibly the only private motor car in picture is the vehicle parked in the shade on the right. The building on the extreme right was a branch office of the Provisional Bank of Ireland.

Bridge Street traffic, 1970

This *Cork Examiner* photograph was taken from a vantage point very close to the previous one, but about forty years later. This is the very same streetscape on 14 July 1970. There has been very little visible change in the street frontage or the skyline, but road traffic has taken over with the resultant gridlock that still bedevils our cities in the early years of the twenty-first century.

Gladys Leach, Cork artist
This 1951 photograph, taken on Patrick Street, shows Mrs Gladys Hyde (*nee* Leach) with two of her children, Stephen and Deirdre. Gladys Leach is well known in Cork artistic circles and is particularly noted for her fine line drawings of Cork buildings, a selection of which were published in 1978 under the title *The Scenery and Character of Cork*. Her drawings have preserved for future reference the look of Cork and its buildings in the latter decades of the twentieth century.